# The Colored Girl
# from
# Long Island

*The story of my early life*

## Sandi Brewster-walker

This edition is published by Lulu Publishers

&

Rams Horn Publishing Company,
Div. of L & P International
8297 Champions Gate Blvd Suite 356
Champions Gate, FL 33896
202-558-7480

Library of Congress Catalog Card Number
$2^{nd}$ printing

ISBN 978-1-4303-0579-8

# DEDICATION

This book is dedicated to my brother Willis Hodges "Hodgie" Brewster, Jr., my father Willis Hodges Brewster, Sr., his father Job(e) Miller Brewster, my father's mother Catherine Imogene Hodges, her father Augustus Michael Hodges, his father Willis Augustus Hodges, and finally Willis' father Charles Augustus Hodges. Our family history and education were extremely important to the Brewsters and Hodges.

In the early 1800s, Charles paid a white woman in Lower Norfolk County, Virginia to teach his children to read and write. Being able to read and write gave Charles' children an advantage over most freemen in Virginia.

Charles' son Willis Augustus Hodges, my great great-grandfather became actively involved in Civil War and Reconstruction politics in Virginia. Willis devoted the better part of his life fighting for justice for the free colored people, and freedom for slaves, as he traveled between Virginia and New York State. With his home-schooled education, Willis started the *Ram's Horn*, the first Black newspaper in Brooklyn, New York. And he wrote his autobiography in the winter of 1848 in a cabin on Loone Lake, New York near John Brown's farm. Willis gave me my love for politics.

Willis' son Augustus Michael Hodges was the first in our family to graduate from college in 1871. He serialized his father's autobiography *Free Man of Color* in the *Indianapolis Freeman* newspaper. And published a column in almost every issue of the newspaper from the 1880s to his death in 1916 under his pen name "B. Square." I got my love of books and writing from Augustus.

Augustus' daughter Catherine Imogene Hodges, my grandmother married Job(e) Miller Brewster, a Long Island Native American with a rich heritage. Catherine died soon after my birth, and my Native ancestors believe that when there is a birth, there is a death. I was the individual that replaced her on this earth to record our history and carry on the morals, as well as the values of our ancestors.

My grandfather Job(e) Miller Brewster knew more than most historians the importance of his Native American heritage, and the significant of his life. His people after three centuries of adjusting to the Dutch and English settlers from 1500 to 1800 had found some peace and prosperity in the hamlet of North Amityville. He wanted his children, grandchildren and great-grand children to know what his people had given up slowly. They had given up 1,400 square miles of land on Long Island.

Catherine and Jobe's son Willis "Bill" Hodges Brewster, Sr., my father was ahead of his time in business, and the golf industry. Bill in the late 1940s and 1950s owned a small business, before society had adjusted to colored business owners. He also followed his dream of playing golf and obtained a single digit handicap, but new he could never enter the world of professional golfers. But, he taught his four (4) daughters and son to follow their dreams.

My brother Willis Hodges "Hodgie" Brewster, Jr., who struggled for his own independence separate from that of his four sisters, once, asked "when did his sisters get it." Well Hodgie, I got it when I began to understand the significance of our heritage, and I think you also get it too! To be able to ask the question proves that you understand the struggle of our ancestors and why we each pass through history. I believe your reason for being and for passing through history was to protect your "four sisters".

You, my brother were my hero, once, even my Santa Claus on Christmas!

I remember the Christmas of 1970, the Vietnam Conflict was being fought somewhere in Southeast Asia, and the Black Revolution was being fought on the streets of America. You, Hodgie were in the U. S. Armed Services stationed at Fort Polk, Louisiana, and we did not think you would be home for the holidays. Outside of the house, like all of Long Island, our street was covered with a blanket of snow dumped from heaven. Inside around midnight, I was trying all by myself to put together my children's toys and had just sat on the couch and began crying in frustration. Sometime after midnight, you knocked on my door!

I never told you, but you were my Santa Claus that year, as you made sure all of the children's toys were assembled.

# ACKNOWLEDGEMENTS

I am grateful for the people, who over the years have encouraged me to write. I am particularly grateful to a few of them for their encouragement, assistance and discussion. I would like to give a special thanks to my ex-husband, Stuart M. Walker for helping me shape my life. He along with my three children -- Jeffrey, Carlton, and Cassandra -- endured many research trips that we called vacations.

A historian, who encouraged me to research, was the late John Blassingame, a professor at Yale University, who was a friend. Over the years, Blassingame and I had numerous discussions about the black experience, and he gave me access to his Frederick Douglas Collection at Yale University.

Thanks goes to David Palmquist, former director and librarian of Special Collections at the Bridgeport Public Library with whom, I was co-director of the Bridgeport Black History Project. The project was an attempt to compile and collate historical information about blacks in Bridgeport between 1790 and 1900.

During this period, I worked as a manufacturing engineer for the division of Perkin-Elmer in Norwalk that built chromatography instruments. The company highlighted the Bridgeport Project on the cover of their annual report. After this project, I knew there were many more stories about the black experience that should be told and that I would tell them.

I also wish to express gratitude to my friends in the City of Stamford, Connecticut a special thanks. There are no words that can describe the value of the support and knowledge that I gained from such people as Harold Wheeler, Jr., former president, Ronald Marcus, librarian, and John Brown, a former board member, all members of the Stamford Historical Society. Wendy Brannen, Yvonne Hill, Jennifer McAllister, Marvin Minkler, and the late Bill Macklin, friends that would listen to me talk about history.

And a very special thanks to my good friend Sid Cassese, a writer and editor on Long Island for helping with my manuscript. I wish to acknowledge the countless individuals, organizations, and companies, who so generously offered ideas, information and support. And thanks goes to my family and friends on Long Island.

Finally, thank you to the numerous historical societies, libraries and city hall staff that assisted me on my many research trips, and search for primary sources.

**Sandi Brewster-walker**

# ABOUT THE AUTHOR

Sandi Brewster-walker is a historian, genealogist, freelance writer, and business owner born in Copiague, NY. She relocated from Connecticut to Northern Virginia at the beginning of President William Jefferson Clinton's Administration. Sandi joined the Clinton Administration in 1993, and was appointed Deputy Director of the Office of Communications at the United States Department of Agriculture. However, she later served as director of the Empowerment Zone and Enterprise Community Program. Towards the end of President Clinton's second term, she moved to historical Williamsburg, Virginia, and a few years later to Florida.

Brewster-walker has taught American History in the secondary education public school system, as well as served an (Acting) Assistant Director for the Urban Center for Black Studies at Vassar College.

Sandi has researched African and Native American genealogy for more than 40-years. Thirty years was spent on researching her great-great grandfather Willis A. Hodges of Princess Anne County, Virginia. Hodges represented Princess Anne County during the Reconstruction Period after the Civil War. She has developed the Invisible People Series, which includes Fairfield County (Connecticut), Lower Norfolk County / Virginia Beach (Virginia), and Suffolk County (New York). Sandi has taught genealogy classes throughout the United States. For three years, she taught black genealogy at the Lloyd House in Alexandria, Virginia for the Fairfax Public School System. She has lectured in New York State, Connecticut, Florida, and Virginia, as well as the University of Connecticut Campus in Stamford, Connecticut.

Brewster-walker is an African American that is highly educated, and a veteran of corporate America. She has been published in a number of national newspapers and magazines, as well as been the subject of feature articles in the *Washington Post*, *Connecticut Post*, *Stamford Advocate*, and *Essence Magazine*.

**Long Island**

# Chapter 1

# The Island

Officially Long Island is 1,400 square miles and extends 120-miles east into the Atlantic Ocean, the second largest of the world's five oceans. It is boarded on the south by the Great South Bay with its off-shore barrier islands, the north by the Long Island Sound, then Connecticut, and the west by the mouth of the muddy formerly blue Hudson River.

The original owners entrusted with the care of Long Island were Indians, however when I was young they were lumped into a category called "colored people."

Centuries before the Dutch and English settlers arrived, the inhabitances of the island of Seawanhacky (Long Island), as it was known were fisherman, hunters and gatherers, who lived on fish, fowl, game, fruit, and vegetables.

They caught oysters, clams, eels, flounder, bunker fish, and mussels along their sandy shores with woven basket, simple hooks, tongs, and nets made of reeds from the island's sandy white beaches. Many of the Natives dragged rakes along the shallow bay or sound bottom. The water surrounding the Island was so clear; the Natives could wade and see the shell fish on the bottom.

The shellfish were used for their meat, as well as their shells. A hole was placed in a shell, and then they were woven onto belts, necklaces, or used as basic currency (wampum) throughout the Native trade of Long Island and New England.

The Natives gathered wild strawberries, blackberries, rhubarb, herbs and roots, as well as planted crops of wild corn, sweet potatoes, squash and beans. Many of the wild roots were used as medicine to cure the sick. However, their wild roots could not fight off the European smallpox.

They used the tiny bunker fish or Atlantic Menhaden, a member of the oily herring family for food, bait and away from the shores as a fertilizer for their crops. By planting one fish with each seed in the spring, they were assured of a rich crop in the fall.

On the eastern end of the Island, the Natives hunted for whales in the Atlantic Ocean. Later, the English settlers gave the Indians the rights to any whales that wash ashore, because the fins and tails of the whales were highly prized for use in their religious ceremonies.

Depending on the seasons, the Native people of Long Island moved from the Seawanhacky shores into the inner woodlands and swamps, not settling in any specific areas. The entire island was their home!

They traded with other coastal Native clans across the Connecticut River known now as the Long Island Sound, and occasionally went to war with the Pequots or other New England tribes. The Natives' lives would drastically change after the European conquerors and then the settlers came spreading smallpox.

The first recorded contact with the Natives at the western end of the Island was with the European explorer Giovanni Verrazzano. The Florentine explorer Giovanni Verrazzano known as Giovanni da Verrazzano was born in or around 1485 at his family's castle *Castello Verrazzano* near Val di Greve, 30 miles south of Florence, Italy. About 1506/7 as a young man, he moved to Dieppe, France to pursue a maritime career.

In 1524/5 King François (Francis I), premier of France commissioned an expedition backed by a wealthy Italian bankers and merchants living in Lyons to investigate the area between the Spanish discovery of Florida, and the English and Portuguese discovery of Newfoundland. Most history books give the date of this expedition, as either 1524 or 1525, which one is correct is lost to time.

King Francois I provided Verrazzano with four ships, and on January 17, 1524/5, Verrazzano departed for his 44-day Atlantic Ocean crossing from Madeira arriving at Cape

Fear, North Carolina around March 1. However two of the boats were shipwrecked shortly after departure. The third was sent home carrying the prizes from privateering on the Spanish coast. The fourth, the flagship *La Dauphine* with a crew of fifty men including his brother Girolamo da Verrazzano, who was a mapmaker actually made the crossing of the Atlantic Ocean.

Next he sailed south, but returned just north of Charleston for fear of running into the Spanish. He then sailed north along the coast reaching the Outer Banks of Carolina. At the area that would become Kitty Hawk, out of curiosity or to prove his expedition, he is said to have kidnapped a young male Indian child, but failed to kidnap a young woman before sailing further north.

It was common for the explorers to plunder and rape their captives. The women and the young men would become the sailors' "bed warmers."

The early explorers kidnapped Indians from coastal communities taking them back to Europe, where they were sold into slavery. As early as 1500, Portuguese explorers went ashore somewhere on the North Atlantic Coast grabbing 57 Indians and taking them back to Portugal, where they were sold on the auction block. Two years later, English sailors landed at Newfoundland, kidnapped three Indian men as proof they had made land. In July 1525, Spanish explorers abducted 58 Indian men and women near what is now Newport, R.I., and brought them back to Spain.

Keeping away from the coastal shoreline Verrazzano for fear of being sighted missed the entrances to Chesapeake and Delaware Bays. He continued north and arrived west of Long Island in the New York Harbor. His journal described briefly the Natives:

*"The people excel us in size: they are of bronze color. Some inclining more to whiteness. Others to tawny color: the face sharply cut. Their hair long and black. Upon which they bestow the greatest study in adorning it: The eyes black and alert. The bearing kind and gentle."*

He anchored in the now New York Harbor.

*"The people are almost like unto the others, and clad with feather of fowls of diverse colors. They came towards us very cheerfully, making great shouts of admiration, showing us where we might come to land most safely with our boat,"*

Leaving the New York Harbor he sailed pass the Island of Shells (Long Island) and eventually left it behind, but observed an offshore island (Block Island), which he named "Louiza" after the Queen of France. It is not known if Verrazzano went a shore onto the Island of Shells.

The second explorer to see the Island of Shells was Henry Hudson. In 1609, the English navigator Henry Hudson on his ships the *Half Moon* made an extensive exploration of the Island of Hills (Manhattan) and part of the Island of Shells (Long Island). The Dutch later claimed the area based on Hudson's voyage.

On the morning of Sept. 6, 1609, Henry Hudson ordered a group of men including an Englishman named John Coleman to go ashore. Coleman or Colman stepped into the small boat and began to paddle toward the shoreline on the far side of the Island of Hills narrows towards *Lange Eylandt* (Long Island). A Hudson's mate, Robert Juet, later wrote, "*the men got into a fight with a group of Indians.*" Later Colman was found with an arrow shot into his throat. The next day Hudson took a group of men ashore to a point of land he named Coleman's Point, and buried the seaman.

The third explorer to sail to the Island of Shells was Adrian Block, a Dutchman in his newly built vessel in 1613. He sailed up the East River through Hell's Gate, then eastward down the length of the Long Island Sound. Proceeding east he entered a large freshwater river he called the ``Fresh River'' (Connecticut River), then rounded the North Fork of Long Island and dropped anchor on the bay side of the South Fork. He named it Hoeck van de Visschers, or Point of the Fishers (Montauk Point).

Once he saw the open ocean behind this point, Block knew that this land mass was an island. He had now been completely around it, and he claimed it all for the Dutch.

It is believed that Block's men made a landing on Montauk Point. Just where has never has been determined, or the length of their stay. The one document that could give us the answers, "Block's own journal" never has been found.

The Dutch and the English began to move to the island of shells wanting more and more of the Island's rich farm land.

By the 1650s, the Native Americans were pushed further inland away from their beautiful white sandy beaches. Consequently, many Natives settled or hid in the swamps like those of the North Amityville hamlet on the east side of what is now Albany Avenue. The Natives were safe here from the greed of the Dutch and English.

Despite the fact that the Natives did not know the land customs and laws of the Dutch and English, nor could they read or write either language, their marks the "x" traded away forever their magnificent island.

By the 1700s, the fanatic Dutch and English, who fled Europe because of religious persecution, or had been exiled because of crime, divided the island with a line that is visible today. The English took and settled what is now known as

Suffolk County, and the Dutch claimed the land from Suffolk County to the far west end of the island that became Queens.

Townships were established that ran from the Long Island Sound on the North shore to the Great South Bay on the South shore. The Town of Easthampton, Southampton, Brookhaven, Huntington, Oyster Bay, and Hempstead began to organize on the land that was traded or stolen from the Natives for items like friendship, two coats, ten pounds of powder, knives, twenty hatchets, etc.

For almost, a 190 years, the settler used slaves to do their hard work, cook, and take care of their children. Many of the settlers had brought their blacks and Native slave with them or purchased some upon arrival on the Island.

Finally, a New York State Legislature Act was passed in 1799 providing for the gradual emancipation of black and Native slaves to set them free on condition of the slave being under fifty years of age, and being capable of supporting himself or herself.

A few of these newly manumitted slaves migrated to the area between the Town of Huntington and the future Incorporated Village of Amityville joining the local Natives that lived in the swamps. Even though they lived independently, the new freedmen worked for some of the same families that had enslaved them. Consequently, the hamlet of North Amityville began to take shape with its colored people.

Non-English or Dutch European immigrants, newly manumitted slaves, black freedmen, and the Natives that originally owned Long Island were now "colored people."

The large townships were slowly being divided into small towns and villages.

According to the Amityville Historical Society in 1836, Amityville was made up of 75 homes, two general stores, two mills, a blacksmith, stage stop, shoe shop, tavern, school, church, and 117 school age children.

Fifty-eight years later, the Incorporated Village of Amityville was organized on March 3, 1894 out of the part of the Town of Huntington called Huntington West Neck South. And the boundary lines were drawn, so that the colored people in the swamps were not included.

North Amityville was born out of the forbidden swamps sandwiched in between the Incorporate Village of Amityville, and the Town of Huntington.

Eventually for political reasons, North Amityville was handed off to the Town of Babylon.

North Amityville was just an area that the Township of Babylon claimed, because neither the Town of Huntington nor the Village of Amityville wanted the land, or its colored people, when the Village of Amityville was incorporated.

Regardless, this is the world of generations of my colored Long Island ancestors.

Finally, my story is about my early life as a colored girl on Long Island, my ancestors, and the segregated society where I grew up.

# Chapter 2

# My Ancestor's Race

Before I tell you about my life, I must first tell you how my ancestor's race was determined by the U. S. Federal Government.

My colored Long Island ancestors' race was distorted by the U. S. Federal Census enumerators, and the instructions they were given by their employer the Federal government. Many individuals were reported as black, colored, or white when in fact they should have been reported as another race or Indian.

The racial identity of blacks or Indians varied from census to census, and from enumerator to enumerator. Different enumerators made conflicting judgments about my relatives, and societies' racial attitudes at the time also influenced the enumerators.

The 1790 Federal census, which was extremely important to the new United States for counting population, and determining representation counted very few of my Native, and black relatives after the American Revolution. Both Indians and blacks became the invisible people!

The limits on the race category in the early census (1790 – 1850) made it impossible for Indians to be reported correctly. From 1800 to 1820, the enumerator recorded my Indian ancestors as either black or white in the race category, if they were counted at all.

It was not until 1860 a new category "civilized Indians" for race was added mainly targeted at the Indians in the westward territories living among the general "white" population. The use of the word "civilized" reflected the attitudes of the country towards Indians.

Finally "civilized" was dropped, the first Federal census to instruct enumerators to use "Indian" as a race classification was the 1880 census.

Blacks had been on Long Island, since the first Dutch and European settlers arrived. And the Dutch West India Company in 1626 began to actively transport African slaves to Long Island. Eleven blacks or "company Negroes" were transported, while Peter Miniut was the Dutch Governor of New York.

Many of my black ancestors were counted statistically as "other free people" or "slaves" in the 1790 to the 1810 Federal census. However, the 1820 census was the first to report some of my relatives in the new "free colored" category.

In New York State in 1821, the legislature enacted a new constitution under its terms black males owning $250 in taxable property were eligible to vote. If the state government taxed you, they counted you!

The Federal census did not change much in 1830 and 1840, but it was still missing many of my Native and black relatives. The enumerator did not feel safe going into the Native or colored sections of a rural community.

In 1850, the enumerator's instructions stated that the "color" of each person (skin) would be reported not their race, and the terms that were used were white, black, colored, or mulatto. And mulatto would include quadroons, and octoroons. This census also created the "slave schedules," which mainly identified my southern slave relative by age, just a few names found their way into the schedules.

When the enumerators went to work on the 1860 and 1870 Federal population census and slave schedule, their instructions on race had not changed.

By the 1890s, after Reconstruction had ended the "grandfather clause," poll tax, and numerous other regulations began to filter out blacks from the voting booths, as well as the census. And the enumerators were asked to look at an individual and determine their blood ratio: white, black, Negro, mulatto (1/2 Negro blood), quadroon (1/4 Negro blood), octoroon (1/8 Negro blood), or Indian. The race of my ancestors was placed in the hands of an enumerator, who spent maybe five-minutes in their home.

The 1900 Federal census used white, black (Negro descent), and Indians as its race categories.

The 1910 and the 1920 census were determine to find anyone passing for white, so the enumerator's instructions stated that a "person with mixed white, and negro blood was considered Negro. And "a person part Indian and Negro should be listed as Negro, unless the Indian blood predominated, and the person was generally accepted as Indian in their community." However, persons with mixed Indian, and white blood were considered Indian. This was the year that the Federal government officially determined that Indians should have "white" skin.

For 140 years, the Federal census enumerators were given the authority to determine the race of my ancestors.

In my story the terms *Black* and *Indian* are used because this is how I refer to my family and race, however I also use the term *colored* since this is how we were known by white America.

Source: The triangle in the Village of Amityville
www.amityvillehistoricalsociety.com

# Chapter 3

# My Birth

On December 7, 1941, my older sister Phyllis was being christened at the Bethel African Methodist Episcopal Church parsonage on the corner of Smith Street and Albany Avenue in North Amityville. This was the same parsonage where my parents were married by Rev. James Henry Thomas and his niece my mother's best friend Benny Nelson (Henry), who stood up with them.

While my sister was being christened, my parents heard on the radio about the attack on democracy. Not long after Pearl Harbor was bombed in Hawaii, I was born in Copiague Lakeside Hospital, as the second child in the marriage of Willis Hodges Brewster nicknamed Bill, and Florence Wilda Scurlock.

My father's parents were Job Miller Brewster and Catherine Imogene Hodges. And my mother's parents were Alberta Fowler Jackson and Edgar Aaron Scurlock. Both Job Brewster and Alberta Jackson were descendents of historic Long Island Indian tribes, as well as freemen, freedmen, slaves, and Europeans. And Catherine Imogene Hodges and Edgar Aaron Scurlock descended from Southern freedmen, slaves, Europeans, and Indians.

However, I was raised in the integrated little hamlet called North Amityville. Here white European immigrants lived on one end of most streets, and the rest of the colored people at the other end.

Most of the descendants of the original Dutch and English settlers lived on the south side of the Long Island Railroad tracks in the Incorporate Village of Amityville.

Traveling North, as you crossed the railroad tracks the white families became poorer as Broadway went left and Albany Avenue began on the right. As Albany Avenue neared Dixon Ave., the white families disappeared and colored families appeared, and the Incorporated Village of Amityville ended and North Amityville began.

However, if you took the left road from the village the families would remain white all the way to Huntington on the north shore of Long Island.

The official dividing lines between the Village of Amityville and North Amityville were the Long Island Railroad tracks to the South, where the sidewalks stopped; Broadway to the West and North, and Great Neck Road to the East.

By the end of World War II racism had quietly and successfully divided Amityville into two parts, the Incorporated Village of Amityville for white families, and

North Amityville for the colored families.  Then, GI housing was built in Levittown for white returning soldiers, and in North Amityville, Roneck Park was built for colored veterans.

Developers built Roneck Park on the site of the old Seth Purdy family farm that was sold to Henry and Herman Von Essen in 1916, and then to a development company.

Seth Purdy, Sr., a white man was born on February 9, 1752, and married Phebe Ketchem, a descendant of the original English settlers on March 6, 1781, the same year he began to farm the land on Albany Avenue near Great Neck Road.  He farmed 188 acres of land.

His two sons, Joshua (b. Mar. 3, 1792), and Seth Jr. (b. September 17, 1800) divided the farm around 1860 into two separate farms of one hundred acres, and eighty-eight acres. Their father, Seth, Sr. had died earlier in 1838.

One brother's farm was located just south of Great Neck Road with a 2-1/2 story farm house on Albany Avenue. Behind the farm house was a pond and stream.  The stream ran through the swamps of North Amityville passing the Native Americans, and continued south to the Great South Bay.

Henry Von Essen purchased the farm in 1916 with its two faded old red barns, but only held it four years until it was purchased by a development company. During the 1920s, the Purdy farm house was burned down, but the two red barns stood until the 1940s.

The other Purdy brother's farm was located at Albany Avenue and Great Neck Road on the original 1781 site of Seth Purdy, Sr.'s farm, and consisted of all four corners of the intersection. The Purdy homestead was a two story white clapboard house with a picket fence, two red barns, cow shed, corn crib, chicken cope, and a work house.

Before the depression, Henry Von Essen's brother Herman purchased the farm. I remember seeing Herman's farm, which grew vegetables mainly potatoes, however the farm was sold in the late 1950s, and both farms were replaced with a black veterans' housing development *Roneck Park.*

The location of Seth Purdy, Jr's farm in 1873 is shown on map #1 along with his colored neighbors the Brewsters, Greens, Smiths, Squires, and Millers.

C. (Charles) Brewster and A. (Albert) Brewster lived off Albany Avenue. G. Green, E. (Elbert) Brewster, and I. Smith lived behind Joshua Purdy's property between Bayview Ave. and Great Neck Road.

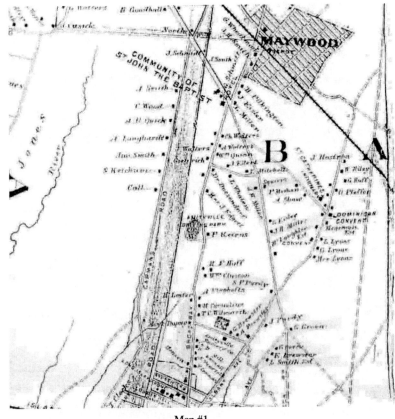

Map #1

Source: 1873 – Map found in the Patchogue–Medford Public Library

North on Great Neck Road was John Henry Miller and the Squire property. The Squire family cemetery is still located off Great Neck Road today.

And the Brewsters, Steeles, Millers, Greens, Smiths, Paynes, Fowlers, and Squires lived side-by-side Joshua Purdy in 1887. The map #2 now showed the AME Church just across Albany Avenue from Joshua Purdy, and further south on Albany Avenue was the Huntington School District #6 Colored School.

Post World War II with the GI Bill in their pocket, the colored veterans living in New York City slowly began to move their families to the working-class Long Island neighborhoods. They were in search of a better life and equal opportunities for their children. However, the veterans would have to learn what the Long Island colored people already knew, the unspoken rules of segregation.

With the building of Levitown and Roneck Park, all of Long Island began to change!

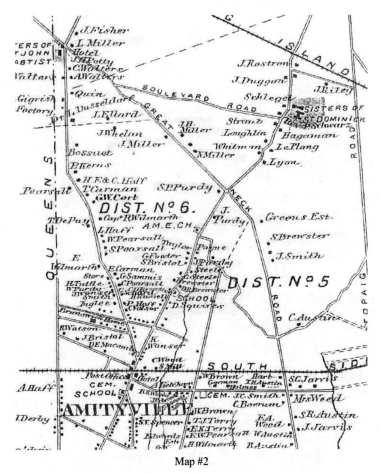

Map #2

Source: 1887 – Map found in the Patchogue–Medford Public Library

# Chapter 4

# Invisible Dividing Line

The waterfront community of the Village of Amityville in 1644 was located on the land that became West Neck South in the Town of Huntington; however the western part is now East Massapequa in the Town of Oyster Bay. East Massapequa was also the site of the largest massacre of Natives on Long Island by the Dutch.

The Dutch Governor William Kieft had hired John Underhill, an Englishman with a reputation of killing Indians in Connecticut. Underhill had become famous during the Pequot Wars. True to his reputation in a place called Fort Neck, Underhill killed 120 Indians in one major battle. His men murdered many of the Indians, and then buried their slaughtered bodies in a mass grave, but some members of the tribe managed to escape into the swamps.

Despite Underhill's effort, a few Indians along with Chief Tackapousha, brother of Chief Wyandance survived only to deed away the rest of their precious land.

When I was born, the surviving Indians great-great-great-great-grandchildren worked for the Dutch and English settler's descendents with names like Ketcham, Tredwell, Platt, Chichester, Conklin, Ireland, and Powell.

My maternal grandmother Alberta Fowler Jackson Scurlock and several great-aunts would cross the invisible dividing line, the Long Island Railroad tracks to go to work as domestics for the white families that lived on the canals of the waterfront communities of Amityville and Massapequa near the Great South Bay.

Grandma Scurlock (b. February 4, 1898) was born out of wedlock to Royal Fowler, a Montauk and Manhasset Indian descendant, and Olive Jackson also an Indian descendant. She never took her father's last name.

Royal Fowler was born in 1875, one of the nine (9) children of George W. Fowler (b. 1837), and Martha Anne Brewster (b. 1838):

      1. George Henry Fowler (b. Dec. 6, 1859-60)

      2. Alexander Fowler (b. 1861-63)

      3. Martha A. Fowler (b. 1864-65)

      4. Hannah E. Fowler Hunter (b. Mar. 1867)

      5. David Fowler (b. Mar. 13, 1869) in Amityville

      6. Emily Fowler (b. 1871) in New York State

      7. John Fowler (b. 1873-75) in New York State

      8. Royal Fowler (b. 1875-76) in New York State

      9. Julia Fowler (b. 1877) in New York State

George Fowler was a Montauk and Manhassett Indian born in East Shinnecock. In the 1860 U. S. Federal Census, he is listed as living with John and Lydia Brewster, his brother-in-law. The next Federal census in 1870 listed George's occupation as a gardener, and then in 1880 as a farmer. He died August 8, 1886 in Amityville.

George was the son of Michael Fowler, a Montauk Indian, and Ellen ____, a Manhassett Indian born on Shelter Island. Ellen was listed as Manhasset referring to the Indian clan living on Shelter Island.

And Royal's mother Martha Anne Brewster was the daughter of Charles Brewster (b. 1809) and Hannah Steele (b. 1806), a mulatto with Long Island Indian roots. She was the sister of my Great-Grandfather Jobe A. Brewster.

Later, Royal married an Adelaide _____ of Bayshore, NY, and finally in 1901 Clara _____ of Wantagh, NY.

# Chapter 5

## Olive Jackson

Grandma Scurlock's mother was Olive Jackson (b. 1877). Olive was born in the colored section of North Bellmore, NY called *Smithville*. She had two children as an unwed mother by Royal Fowler, my Grandmother and her brother Frederick Fowler Jackson. But Olive died young causing her two little children to be raised by her brother Theodore G. Jackson in Bethpage, NY, and the Jackson family in Bellmore.

Olive was one of the six (6) daughters born to William Jackson (b. 1830) and Emelia (Ellen) _____ (b. 1833) on Long Island; however this was William's second marriage. William's first marriage was to a woman named Margaret _____ (b. 1830). I think Margaret might have died, since William and Emelia named their first child Margaret:

1. Sarah Jackson (b. 1857) 1$^{st}$ mar.
2. Theodore G. Jackson (1861-62) 1$^{st}$ mar.
3. Julia Jackson (b. 1863) 1$^{st}$ mar.
4. Emma Jackson (b. 1864) 1$^{st}$ mar.
5. Margaret Jackson (b. 1872)
6. Eliza. A. Jackson (b. 1873)
7. Christine Jackson (b. 1876)

8. Olive Jackson (b. 1877)

9. Laura Jackson (b. 1879)

10. Addie Jackson (b. 1880)

William was enumerated in the 1850 U. S. Federal Census as living in the Town of Oyster Bay, Queens (now Nassau) NY. However, the 1870 census enumerated him in the Town of Hempstead as a farm laborer.

My Grandma Scurlock's brother Frederick Jackson married Florence _____ (Frazier) of Bayshore. He lived for years in Bayshore, but died before I had a chance to meet him. But Grandma Scurlock gave me a picture of her brother in a World War I Army uniform. He had been a member of the 369th infantry regiment called the Harlem Hellfighters.

*Wikipedia*, a free encyclopedia on the Internet states that the 369th Infantry Regiment was constituted June 2, 1913 in the New York Army National Guard as the 15th New York Infantry Regiment and organized on June 29, 1916 at New York City. It was Mustered into Federal service on July 25, 1917 at Camp Whitman, New York, and then drafted into Federal service on August 5, 1917.

The regiment trained in the New York Area, performing guard duty at various locations in New York, and trained more intensely at Camp Wadsworth in Spartanburg, South Carolina, where they experienced significant racism from the local communities, as well as other units. The 15th was assigned on December 1, 1917 to the 185th Infantry Brigade, and commanded by Col. William Hayward, a member of the Union League Club of New York, which sponsored the 369th in the tradition of the 20th U.S. Colored Infantry, which the club had also sponsored during the Civil War.

The 15th shipped out on December 27, 1917, and joined the 185th Infantry Brigade in France, but the unit was relegated to labor service duties instead of combat training. And on January 5, 1918 the Brigade was assigned to the 93rd Division [provisional].

The 15th was reorganized and redesignated March 1, 1918 as the 369th, but the unit continued labor service duties. It was finally decided on April 8, 1918 to assign the unit to the French Army for the duration of the United States participation in the war. The men were issued French helmets and brown leather belts and pouches, although they continued to wear their U.S. uniforms.

The 369th was relieved May 8, 1918 from assignment to the 185th Infantry Brigade, and went into the trenches as part of the 16th French Division and served continuously to July 3rd. The regiment returned to combat in the Second Battle of the Marne. Later the 369th was reassigned to Gen. Lebouc's

161$^{st}$ Division. On August 19, the regiment went off the line for rest and training of replacements. But on September 25, 1918 the 4$^{th}$ French Army went on the offensive in conjunction with the American drive in the Meuse-Argonne, and the 369$^{th}$ joined them. At one point the 369$^{th}$ advanced faster than French troops on their right and left flanks. There was danger of being cut off, but by the time the regiment pulled back for reorganization, it had advanced fourteen kilometers through severe German resistance.

In mid-October the regiment was moved to a quiet sector in the Vosges Mountains, and was there on November 11, the day of the Armistice. Six days later, the 369$^{th}$ made its last advance on November 26 reaching the banks of the Rhine River.

The regiment was relieved on December 12, 1918 from assignment to the French, and returned to the New York City port, and demobilized on February 28, 1919 at Camp Upton at Yaphank, New York. During its service the regiment suffered 1500 casualties and took part in Champagne–Marne, Meuse–Argonne, Champagne 1918, and Alsace 1918 campaigns.

# Chapter 6

## Edgar Aaron Scurlock, Sr.

Edgar Aaron Scurlock, my mother's father was a pale white-skinned colored man with baby blue eyes. It pains me to say, he could pass the "brown paper bag test" in the black community.

Until the 1950s the brown paper bag test was a ritual practiced by some in the black sororities and fraternities to discriminated against people, who they believe were "too dark" for their membership. If, your skin tone was darker than a brown paper lunch bag, you were denied membership.

Grandpa Scurlock was born in the Rockfish section of Fayetteville, North Carolina on January 27, 1891, as one of the five (5) children of Edward K. Scurlock and his wife Mary Jane Lutterloh (Ludlow):

1. Edgar Aaron Scurlock
2. Mary Lille Scurlock Miller
3. Alves Scurlock (b. June 1885)
4. Robert Scurlock
5. Ellen Scurlock Broadnick (b. January 1895).

Cousin Sonny's mother Ellen was the youngest, and one of the first to die, leaving her sister Mary Lille to raise her son Donald Broadnick.

Grandpa Scurlock's father Edward, who never migrated North, was the son of Neil Scurlock and his wife Elizabeth Barge. Neil and Elizabeth had three (3) children:

1. David P. Scurlock
2. George Clay Scurlock
3. Edward Scurlock

Edward K. Scurlock was born between 1851 and 1859, just before the Civil War. He married Mary Jane Lutterloh on October 14, 1879 as the Reconstruction Era was ending the dreams of the freedmen.

Edward died in Fayetteville in 1916 leaving his property and personal items to his children in the North. But, a legal document sent south indicated that his children wanted everything sold.

Mary was one of the three (3) children of John Lutterloh and his wife Ellen Mathews:

1. Mary Jane Lutterloh (b. Sept. 22, 1868)
2. Elizabeth Lutterloh (b. 1871)
3. Joseph Lutterloh (b. 1872)

John Lutterloh was enumerated in the 1850 US Federal Census slave schedule as an eleven year old mulatto slave on the plantation of Thomas S. Lutterloh in the Columbia Township, Randolph County, North Carolina. Whether he was a child of one of the white Lutterlohs and a slave is still in question.

Ellen Mathews, a mulatto was born between 1834 and 1835. She was probably the former slave of April Mathews, a white woman living in Fayetteville. In the 1900 U. S. Federal Census, Ellen was enumerated as a colored servant of Edmond Jennings in Fayetteville. She spent her life around Fayetteville in Cross Creek Township, Cumberland County, North Carolina.

# Chapter 7

# The Great Migration North

Domestic workers, cooks, and chauffeurs had become the largest occupations after the Civil War for colored people on Long Island, as well as in most areas of the country. Colored people and Indians had gained their experience during as slaves or freemen.

After the Civil War, southern ex-slave or freedmen had been hopeful about their future, but with the end of the Reconstruction Era, hundreds of thousands were leaving the South and the "Great Migration" had begun.

My Grandpa Scurlock along with a half million colored people migrated North to escape the intolerable conditions in the South between 1914 and 1915.

Ellen and John Lutterloh's daughter Mary Jane Lutterloh Scurlock joined the Great Migration North leaving her husband Edward Scurlock to come to Long Island to work as a domestic. She left Jim Crow, unemployment, inferior schools, legal injustice, and lynching behind. Mary Jane was not alone, during this period the Leftenant and Wilbourne women left the South for domestic jobs on Long Island.

The Great Migration affected mostly colored women, who were transported in large numbers to the North to serve as domestics and cooks. These women left their own children in the hands of relatives in the South to raise northern white children.

With the rise of the Klu Klux Klan (KKK) popularity, increased lynching, as well as the movie *Birth of a Nation* the racial attitudes of the country were clear as the Great Migration accelerated in 1915 and 1916.

For 30 years from 1888 to 1918, the lynching of colored people increased and became out of control. More than 3, 224 individuals were lynched, and 2,472 were colored males and two were colored females.

Most were lynched for fabricated reasons like using offensive language, bad reputation, refusal to give up their farm or land, throwing stones, unpopularity, illicit distilling, slapping a white child, being troublesome, stealing hogs, or chickens, disagreement with a white man, mistaken identification, murder or rape of a white woman.

And between 1889 and 1916 in North Carolina where my Scurlock relatives lived saw more than 46 colored people and Indians lynched. In my Hodges relatives' Virginia there were more than 77 lynchings. However, lynching was not the only problem plaguing colored people.

In 1915, colored female domestics were being blamed for spreading tuberculosis. At a health convention in Dallas, Texas a white physician unfairly accused colored female domestics of spreading, "the Negro Servant Disease." And white America believed it!

As late as 1918, there were two lynchings in North Carolina and one in Virginia.

Colored people fled the South, but soon discovered that lynching was taking place in the North. In New York State, Robert Lewis, George H. Smith, and Paulo Boleta were some of those lynched.

And on September 8, 1922, a local KKK held a meeting in Freeport, Long Island. White citizens were also actively holding meetings in the home of Mr. Gerring in Roosevelt, and at 59 Babylon Turnpike on the site where an AME Church now stands. On July 4, 1928, the Klan burned a cross in Roosevelt.

But Freeport and Roosevelt were not alone throughout the 1920s, there were numerous KKK parades held in other parts of Long Island.

The number of people being lynched declined during World War II, however they did not stop. In 1946, we saw a slight increase in post war America directed mainly at returning colored veterans. And during the Civil Rights Movement of the 1950s and early 1960s lynching rose again!

The importation of colored women from the South had become a profession for some white entrepreneurs. In almost all northern cities there were agents, who trafficked in supplying colored women as domestic servants and colored men as chauffeurs.

In New York City in 1904, there were more than one hundred agencies trafficking in southern domestics. Three-fourths operated out of living rooms and kitchens of rooming houses.

Mary Jane Scurlock and other colored women would sign contracts at their departure point agreeing to approximately $12 or $14 for transportation by boat plus the cash advancement to an agent. Most would also assign their first month's wages, which were approximately $12 to $20 to the agent. All rights over their personal baggage were signed away to the agent, who would keep the articles until they were paid their fee. And some agents kept the articles as long as they wished to keep control over their colored female domestic.

Similar to the domestic slave trade, agents transported the prospective domestic or chauffeur, paying for their travel

north.    Other agents recruited domestic workers at bus
stations, train stations, and shipping ports in the North.

These colored women were forced into a domestic
slavery similar to prostitution and their agents were no more
than pimps.

The colored domestics were met by a runner similar to
the slave drivers just a short time ago.  The runner would take
the newly indebted domestic to their rooming house or
employer's home.

Agents would inquirer if the new employee had friends,
relative or children old enough to work, later transporting
them.

Mary Jane, a domestic arrived followed by her older
daughters, later her sons followed to be employed as
chauffeurs.  Eventually, all of her children were working as
domestics or chauffeurs in the Northern homes and estates on
Long Island.

The Great Migration gave rise to a new social problem
because colored domestics and chauffeurs were required to
sleep outside their homes, away from their families in their
employer's home.  Some children were sent south and others
were being raised by northern extended families.

Many domestics like my grandfather Edgar and
grandmother Alberta worked for different families leaving

my aging great-grandmother Mary Jane, and my great aunt Mary Lil to raise my mother.

Amityville Beach

Source: www.amityvillehistoricalsociety.com

# Chapter 8

# Segregated Amityville Beach

When I was young, my colored relatives were still chauffeurs, live-ins, and day domestics, who work near the Incorporated Village of Amityville Beach. This segregated village beach had opened on land formerly owned by the Alfred G. Vanderbilt estate in 1940.

Alfred G. Vanderbilt was born in 1877 in New York City, and was the third son of Alice Claypoole Gwynne and Cornelius Vanderbilt II. The Vanderbilt family had acquired some of the best Long Island waterfront property for summer estates. While traveling, Alfred's ship was torpedoed, triggering a secondary explosion that sank the giant ocean liner within eighteen minutes. Vanderbilt and Ronald Denyer, his valet were among the men assisting female passengers into lifeboats, but did not survive the incident. He died May 1, 1915 at sea. For 25-years, his family and estate held onto the Amityville waterfront property before selling it. Later, the property became the Village of Amityville beach.

On Saturday the colored children of North Amityville could take swimming lessons at the village beach, but we had to leave right after our lesson.

The colored people of North Amityville were considered non-residents! God forbid, if the white residents of the Village should swim with a colored person. I always wondered if they drained the Great South Bay after we left!

Unspoken segregated rules of behavior had been negotiated centuries before I was born around the time the Dutch were slaughtering Indians, and the English settlers were tricking them into signing land deeds. And the colored veterans from New York City had not migrated to the area in numbers yet.

I grew up in this segregated society in a controlled environment on the other side of the Long Island Railroad tracks. I was raised in North Amityville, a community where all of the white and colored adults new the rules of segregation.

Catherine Imogene Hodges

# Chapter 9

# Catherine Imogene Hodges

Soon after I was born, my father's mother Catherine Imogene Hodges Brewster died. I feel I was the life that replaced her on earth, as a part of God's plan  She was buried in the back of the Amityville Cemetery in the colored section with only a little medal marker, and her body was interred facing westward in the direction where her soul was thought to travel. This was a Native custom of my Grandpa Job's family.

The tall stately Catherine was born March 19, 1891 in Brooklyn, NY

My father told me that his mother Catherine would attend a church in Harlem, NY.  She also got very upset when my father, as a teenager played trumpet in the Steeplechase Band at Coney Island.  After grandma Catherine found out, my father was only allowed to play the trumpet in her church in New York City.  This ended his career in music!

# Chapter 10

# Augustus Michael Hodges

Catherine's parents were Augustus Michael Hodges and Anna Kennedy. Her father Augustus Michael Hodges, a colored man was born in 1854 in Blackwater, VA., and graduated from high school in Vineland, N. J., Hampton Agricultural & Technical College in 1872, and Werner Latin School. He was a teacher, and later a writer, who grew up between Brooklyn, NY and the Tidewater area of Virginia.

For a short time as a young man, he sailed on a Pacific Mail Steamship under his uncle Labon Walker Corprew's supervision.

Augustus, who taught school in Kempsville, Virginia for a decade, abandoned his position and settled in Brooklyn, where he became active in the Republican Party. He was nominated to represent the United States in Haiti during the early years of President Benjamin Harrison Administration (1889-1893).

Augustus became a popular writer, journalist, and poet, whose columns appeared regularly under his pen name "B. Square." He wrote for the *People's Advocate* (Washington, D. C.), *Christian Recorder* (Philadelphia, PA), *New York Globe* (later known as *the New York Age*), and the

*Indianapolis Freedman.* And he also was editor of *The Sentinel* newspapers in Brooklyn.

Augustus died in the summer of 1916 while living at his daughter Sadie's home at 111 West 135th Street, Harlem, N Y. After his death, his second wife Caroline, who had been born a slave came to North Amityville to live with Catherine's family.

# Chapter 11

# Rev. Willis Augustus Hodges

Augustus' father Rev. Willis Augustus was born on February 12, 1815 to free parents, Charles Augustus Hodges and Julia Nelson Willis. Willis was the second son of Charles and Julia.

Around 1847, Willis was living in Brooklyn, and attending abolitionist meetings. While there, Willis started the first black newspaper in Brooklyn, NY – the *Rams Horn*.

Willis' autobiography *Free Man of Color* tells about how the question of the right of suffrage for blacks was an election campaign issue; and the New York *Sun*, a leading newspaper in an article told it's readers "if they wanted to have a 'nigger' marry into their families and many other objectionable things to vote 'yes', if not to vote 'no.'" Willis prepared a reply to the article, and took it to the editor of the *Sun*. But the editor would not publish it unless Willis paid $15 dollars. Willis paid the $15 dollars, but the editor of the *Sun* put Willis' article down in the corner out of sight of readers. Willis went again to the editor, and demanded to know why. The editor said, "The *Sun* shines for all white men not black men. You must get up a paper of your own if you want to tell your side of the story to the public." And Willis was dismissed by the editor "Good morning."

On January 1, 1847 in New York City Thomas Van Rensselaer, a well-known black abolitionist, and Willis A. Hodges began to publish their newspaper the *Ram's Horn*.

Van Rensselaer and Willis sent hundreds of copies to all the known abolitionists. One of their papers found its way to John Brown, the radical abolitionist, who lived in Springfield, MA. Brown and Willis became good friends. Soon after they both received land owned by Gerrit Smith in upstate New York and Willis moved to Franklin County in the Adirondack Mountains. And John Brown moved near by to Lake Placid.

On October 27, 1847, Willis received from Smith a deed for forty acres of land in the Ninth Township of Franklin County near Loon Lake. During the winter of 1848 and 1849, Brown and Willis corresponded frequently. Five of the letters survived and are in a collection at the Columbia University Library.

Brown would also write his famous satirical essay, "Sambo's Mistake," which appeared in the *Ram's Horn* in 1848. Brown and Willis remained friends after Willis returned from upstate New York to Brooklyn, NY

During the week of February 26 and March 3, 1858, John Brown is reported to have been in Brooklyn on a visit as the guest of Dr. James N. Gloucester, a wealthy black clergyman and abolitionist. During Browns visit he revealed to Gloucester and perhaps his friend Willis his plan to invade Virginia. Consequently, in 1859, John Brown was captured in a raid on Harpers Ferry, West Virginia in route to the Tidewater area of Virginia. And Willis went into hiding for awhile.

Willis Hodges, my Great-Great-Grandfather disappeared from sight between 1859 and 1863, however secretly he was believed to be "Specs Hodges", who made raids on the Confederate forces in May 1862. Several other raids were attributed to "Specs" during the Civil War in the Tidewater area.

Hodges had received the nickname of "specs" because of the large, metal-rimmed glasses he wore. After the Civil War, Willis remained committed to fighting for the rights of black freedmen.

Willis appears again in Brooklyn, NY the summer of 1864 on a mission on behalf of the Virginia freedmen. And on August 9, Willis was at a public meeting held for black citizens of Brooklyn at the church of his' younger brother Charles to discuss the plight of the freedmen.

In September 1864, Willis arrived back in Norfolk where he toured the abandoned farms, Wise and other plantations that were now Freedmen Bureau camps assisting many in their new life. Regardless, Willis and his brothers William, Charles and John Q. were back in their birth state participating actively in Reconstruction politics.

The statewide organization of the Republican Party in Virginia and the enactment of the First Reconstruction Act in 1867 were a signal to Willis, his brothers, and other relatives to become actively involved in party politics. The Hodges brothers spearheaded voter registration drives and spoke often at political rallies.

Willis became a Virginia Reconstruction representative during the Underwood Convention. The Underwood Convention drafted the new constitution of the Commonwealth of Virginia to bring the state back into the Union after the Civil War. In the transcript of the convention, Old Specs as Willis was known is quoted and congratulated for being an eloquent speaker.

Willis also represented Princess Anne County, Virginia at the Republican State Convention in Richmond on August 1, 1867, and served as its vice president. He was now openly known as "Old Specs."

In 1874, he was one of the three justices elected to the Kempsville magisterial district. And in 1877 Willis' twenty-three year old son, Augustus Michael Hodges, my Great Grandfather ran for the state legislature and despite claims of being fairly elected was "counted out" by the Democrats and denied a seat in the Virginia House of Delegates. As Reconstruction ended, members of the Hodges family left Virginia and returned to New York.

With all hopes gone and Reconstruction a thing of the past, Willis moved back to Brooklyn in 1881, but missed Virginia, so he returned in 1885 to the outskirts (Chesapeake) of Norfolk.

Willis and his wife Sarah Ann Corprew had six (6) children that lived:

1. Willis Emanuel Hodges (died as a young child)
2. Willis F. Hodges
3. Augustus Michael Hodges (b. 1854)
4. Kattie J. Hodges (b. 1856)
5. Victoria Hodges (b. 1859)
6. Pinkey L. Hodges (b. 1863)

Sarah Ann Corprew was born 1822 in Virginia, but died April 23, 1890 in Brooklyn, NY. She is buried in the Cyprus Hills Cemetery in Queens on Long Island.

Willis' wife Sarah was a widow and the daughter of John Walker Corprew, a slave owned by John Walker, the owner of the Walker Plantation in Virginia, and her mother Sarah Ann _____ born 1801. The Corprew family had four (4) children:

1. Labon Walker Corprew, Jr.
2. Catherine Corprew
3. Alexander P. Corprew (lost at sea)
4. Sarah Ann Corprew.

Both Labon, Jr. and Alexander became merchant seaman.

Their mother Sarah died in 1889. Her mother was a young girl born in Guinie, West Africa. She was brought on a slave ship to the American colonies. I consider her a survivor, who had endured the harsh trip from West Africa. When she was shipped, millions of Africans were being sold into slavery.

From the slave fort dungeons in West Africa, this young girl became an unwilling participant in the Atlantic slave trade. Many of the Africans died in the crowed cells and others committed suicide aboard the ships. Those that were left suffered from starvation and disease.

On September 24, 1890, Willis died at the age of seventy-five. For a complete survey of Willis Augustus Hodges's life read *Free Man of Color* his autobiography.

Because of my father's mother Catherine family – the Hodges, I have been lucky to inherit strong Virginia blood, and an activist drive to right the injustices of people of color.

# Chapter 12

## Charles Augustus Hodges

Willis' father was Charles Augustus Hodges born free in 1776 in Blackwater, VA. His mother Sarah Cuffee (b. 1745-1751) was a free woman making her children free. But Charles' father was a slave on a Hodges plantation.

At the age of twelve, Charles worked two days in the week in his father's place for the slave master, so that his father might be home one day. Later he worked in place of his elderly father, so the older man would not have to work, and finally purchased his fathers' freedom.

Charles Hodge, a farmer had been married just a few years, when his 1$^{st}$ wife died in childbirth leaving him to raise James, his son. James married Patsy Turner, a granddaughter of the famous Nat Turner.

At the age of 26, Charles married his second wife a young woman named Julia Nelson Willis, a free mulatto the daughter of Sarah Nelson, a white woman and William Willis, her father's black slave. Julia was born 1787 in Princess Anne County, Virginia.

Charles and Julia had twelve (12) children that lived:

1. Julia N. Hodges
2. Hannabel Hodges

3. Georgia "Freby" Hodges

4. Elizabeth Hodges

5. Cordellia Hodges

6. Soffia Hodges

7. William Johnson Hodges (b. 1803)

8. Jaqueline Hodges (b. 1810)

9. Sarah A. Hodges (b. 1813 – 1822)

10. Willis Augustus Hodges (b. February 12, 1815)

11. Charles E. Hodges (b. May 1819)

12. David E. Hodges (1823-24)

Once Charles registered as a free black in Princess Anne County, VA, and is described as being 5' 8" tall and 55-years of age. The freeman's registration stated, he was a bright mulatto, and had a scar on the first joint of his forefinger of his right-hand.

Sarah Nelson was the daughter of Charles and Julia Nelson (Neilson) born in England. They immigrated first to the West Indies, then Florida, South Carolina and finally settling in Princess Anne County (Virginia Beach), Virginia.

There was once a British Mercantile claim against Charles Nelson (Neilson) for indigo seed production in South Carolina. And on October 22, 1779, the House of Delegates in Virginia discharged Charles Nelson (Neilson) from confinement, where he was ordered by resolution of the convention in May 1776. His estate was restored, however Charles died in prison.

In 1810, Charles Hodges purchased on installments the Casteen Farm in Norfolk County, VA, but after he made improvements, his young family was forced off the land.

Charles acquired about another 200 acres of land in Princess Anne County between 1835 and 1840. However after his death in 1844, the Hodges family's white neighbors began to give them trouble. Shortly after 1851, a slave patrol ran his family off their land, but the Hodges kept returning. The slave patrols later became the Klu Klux Klan.

Despite the fact that education was illegal for blacks in Virginia, Charles and Julia understood its importance, and arranged for their older children to be taught to read and write by a white woman named Wilson, who is believed to be a relative.

The Hodges lived a quiet life until around the time of the Nat Turner War. Armed with the ability to read and write, Charles's second son, William Johnson Hodges became a bold critic of slavery and the discrimination against free people of color. He became "exhorter," a preacher who boldly articulated the aspirations of the blacks. William practiced what he preached by forging "free papers" for slaves.  He was arrested, but with assistance from abolitionist escaped to Canada.

This was the Hodges family's first encounter with the abolitionist and the Underground Railroad.  However, William returned from Canada to Brooklyn, NY, and later his beloved Virginia.

# Chapter 13

# Sarah Cuffee

Charles' mother Sarah Cuffee was born between 1745 and 1751. She appears in John Curling's household in the District of Edmonds Bridge, VA in 1761 as taxable. By 1765, she was taxable in the household of William Sikes.

Her mother was also named Sarah Cuffee (b. 1725 – 1732), and was taxable property in 1759 in John Curling's household.

The older Sarah Cuffee had five (5) children:

1. Dinah Cuffee
2. John Cuffee (b. 1743)
3. Sarah Cuffee (b. 1745 – 1751)
4. Rachel Cuffee (b. 1753)
5. Charles Cuffee (b. 1755)

In Norfolk County on March 19, 1763, a court had the older Sarah's children bound out as apprentice to Ruth Gamman. And in 1767 in the District of Great Bridge, Norfolk County, she was listed as a free Negro living in Virginia, but was taxable along with her sister Mary Cuffee and Ann Smith.

The older Sarah's father was John Cuffee, but my research has not uncovered her mother's name.

# Chapter 14

## John Cuffee

John Cuffee, a black man was born in Virginia, as mentioned I have not found his wife's name, but believe it was Sarah. They had five (5) children:

1. George Cuffee
2. Sarah Cuffee (b. 1725 – 1732)
3. John Cuffee (b. 1730 – 1743)
4. Mary Cuffee (b. 1735 – 1740)
5. John, the first John probably died as a child (b. 1772)

On September 18, 1718, John brought a charge against a Robert Taylor, a white man for assault and battery.

Mr. Taylor delayed the case each time it was called, and then on August 19, 1719 Taylor died. John on November 18, 1719 brought another suit against the Taylor estate. When the suit finally made it to court on May 18, 1720, it had been rewritten as a suit for John Cuffee's freedom. However, the case was dismissed because John left his family and the Tidewater area of Virginia in fear for his life.

His parents were John Cuffee, Sr. born 1690, and Jemina. John, Sr. was referred to as "my Negro Coffee" in an appeal to the Virginia court system, however his case was dismissed. He is also mentioned in the Will of James Burtell (Burwell) of the old site of Elizabeth City, VA on September 10, 1716.

Another or the same Cuffee ran away from the King's Creek plantation owned by the grandson of Lewis Burwell II. The runaway crossed the James River by boat into Norfolk County.

Jemina is only mentioned as having a value of 30 pounds in 1746 by Nathaniel Bacon.

Since the late 1600s, the Cuffee and Hodges family have lived in the Tidewater area of Virginia.

Irish Immigrants

www.spartacus.schoolnet.co.uk

# Chapter 15

# Irish Immigrants

My paternal grandmother Catherine's mother Anna Kennedy was born in August between 1860 and 1867 in Ireland just after the "great famine." Anna with her mother Ann, sisters Cath (Catherine), and Marg (Margaret) boarded at Albert Dock, and sailed on the SS Manhattan ship from Liverpool, England in 1876. The ships were so crowded they were named "coffin ships."

She arrived at Castle Clinton (Castle Garden) in the Battery area of New York City, too early for the Ellis Island experience, but probably settled in a "shanty town" with her family.

Castle Clinton was the New York State immigration station from 1855 to 1890. When Anna arrived the station was ill-equipped and unprepared for the eight million immigrants that disembarked, and were dumped into the category of colored people.

Anna probably arrived as a third class passenger because her mother was listed as a "spinster" on the manifest of the steerage section of the ship. But their immigration records were moved in 1892 to the new Ellis Island

Immigration Station, which had a fire on June 14, 1897 destroying many of the earlier records dating back to 1855. Anna's lost individual record would have given her genealogical information.

Life for the new Irish immigrants was hard, as soon as their boat docked agents and runners, who were some of the same men that would later traffic in colored domestics, boarded the ships. These men grabbed at the immigrants, their families and bags, forcing the arrivals to selected rooming houses, and then requiring a large fee.

The new immigrant had no means of moving on, so most settled in or near their port of arrival. Almshouse (poor houses) began to fill with unemployed Irish immigrants, since advertisements for work would include "no Irish need apply." The hard life for immigrants caused Anna's family to leave the New York for Nova Scotia, and a better life.

Large numbers of Irish families were settling in Canada. However, somehow at the age of 20 or 21, Anna made her way back to New York City in 1880, and worked as a servant or chamber maid until meeting her husband.

Others with the name of Kennedy had arrived on the same ship the SS Manhattan:

**Data Source: New York Passenger Lists, 1820-1957**

| Name | Arrival | Estimated birth year | Gender | Port of Departure | Place of Origin |
|---|---|---|---|---|---|
| Ann Kennedy | 23 Dec 1872 | abt 1844 | Female | Liverpool | England |
| Anna Kennedy | 23 Dec 1872 | abt 1867 | Female | Liverpool | England |
| Capt Kennedy | 23 Dec 1872 | abt 1842 | Male | Liverpool | England |
| Cath Kennedy | 23 Dec 1872 | abt 1865 | Female | Liverpool | England |
| Christina Kennedy | 23 Dec 1872 | abt 1861 | Female | Liverpool | England |
| Danl Kennedy | 23 Dec 1872 | abt 1821 | Male | Liverpool | England |

7 – Pages of passengers.

Source Information:
Ancestry.com. New York Passenger Lists, 1820-1957 [database on-line]. Provo, UT, USA: MyFamily.com, Inc., 2006. Original data:
- New York. Passenger Lists of Vessels Arriving at New York, New York, 1820-1897. Micro-publication M237. Rolls # 1-675. National Archives, Washington, D.C.
- New York. Passenger and Crew Lists of Vessels Arriving at New York, New York, 1897-1957. Micro-publication T715. Rolls # 1-8892. National Archives, Washington, D.C.

Description:
This database is an index to the passenger lists of ships arriving from foreign ports at the port of New York from 1820-1957. In addition, the names found in the index are linked to actual images of the passenger lists. Information contained in the index includes given name, surname, age, gender, arrival date, port of arrival, port of departure and ship name.

Augustus M. Hodges, the writer and Anna married in 1885, and had three children:

1. Willis A. Hodges

2. Sarah Hodges (b. 1887)

3. Catherine I. Hodges Brewster ( (March 19, 1891)

The story is told how two of Anna's sisters came to Brooklyn, NY to visit Anna and her new husband, the successful writer. Discovering her husband was "colored," they sat on their trunks until sunrise.

**SS Manhattan, Guion Line**

| Burden | Built | | | Shipowner or operator | Dimensions |
|---|---|---|---|---|---|
| 2,869 gross | 1866 at Jarrow-on-Tyne by Palmer's Shipbuilding & Iron Co. Ltd. | | | Guion Line | 335ft x 42.5ft |

| Year | Departure | Arrival | | Remarks |
|---|---|---|---|---|
| 1866 | | | | May 15, launched |
| 1866 | | | | Aug. 8, maiden voyage Liverpool - Queenstown - New York |
| 1870 | Liverpool | New York | Oct. 16 | < TD> |
| 1872 | Liverpool | New York | May 15 | Agent DHrr. Blichfeldt & Co., Christiania < TD> |
| 1872 | Liverpool | New York | June 25 | < TD> |
| 1872 | Liverpool | New York | Aug. 19 | < TD> |
| 1872 | Liverpool | New York | Sept. 29 | < TD> |
| 1872 | Liverpool | New York | Nov. 05 | < TD> |
| 1874 | | | | Rebuilt: fitted with compound engines by Fawcett & Preston, Liverpool, new tonnage: 3,231 gross |
| 1875 | | | | Jan. 20, chartered by American Line for one vaoyage Liverpool - Philadelphia |
| 1875 | | | | Sold to Warren Line, renamed Massachusetts |
| 1881 | | | | Renamed City of Lincoln for Thistle Line |
| 1881 | | | | Renamed City of Lincoln for Cassels, London |
| 1884 | | | | Renamed Solis for Spanish owners |
| 1902 | | | | Wrecked near Cape Town |

The information listed above is not the complete record of the ship. The information was collected from a multitude of sources, and new information will be added as it emerges

They never returned to the house in Brooklyn where the colored man lived with their sister. To this day, we know very little about the Kennedy family of Ireland and Nova

Scotia, and they know very little about the well-respected Hodges family of Virginia and New York.

On September 8, 1909, Annabella Solomon married Willis A. Hodges, the son of Augustus and Anna in one of the most fashionable weddings in New York City's black community at the Saint Philip's Protestant Episcopal Church.

Annabella is believed to be the daughter of the President of Haiti. After the wedding reception and before the couple departed on their wedding trip, Augustus Hodges presented the couple with a packet of letters from John Brown to the groom's grandfather Willis A. Hodges.

Anna died July 6, 1896 at 37/38 years old, and Augustus became a "single father. My grandmother Catherine was just 5-years old. Augustus lived in Brooklyn and New York City until his death in 1916.

Job Miller Brewster as a chauffeur.

# Chapter 16

# Job Miller Brewster

My Grandmother Catherine Imogene Hodges married Job Miller Brewster.   Job was born July 5, 1889 in Amityville, NY, and was a descent of a number of the historic Long Island Native tribes.   His parents were Job(e) Valentine Brewster and Cornelia Frances Miller.

He was a professional chauffeur as a young man, later drove 30-years for U. S. Trucking Company in New York City until retirement in 1959.

Before Job married Catherine in 1913, he built a house at 63 Brewster Lane just next door to his father's farm. The house was built without electricity or an inside bathroom.

Catherine was a city girl and the country was too backwards for her, so the new married couple spent the winters in Brooklyn and returned in the summer to North Amityville, only if they did not go to Sag Harbor.   Fred, their oldest child was born the same year the couple married.

Fred was sickly and Catherine preferred to be near the city hospitals, as well as her church in Harlem.  Her second child, Sarah was moved back and forth between the country and city families. However by this time my father Willis Hodges Brewster, Sr., nicknamed Bill was born November

27, 1918 in Harlem Hospital in New York City; the young family was spending most of their time in their in the country. Grandpa went back to his farming roots, and began to raise chickens, grow vegetables, as well as taking a second job of growing Dahlias flowers. For years long with his young sons, Grandpa would sell the flowers at the New York City Flower Market down by the New York City docks.

As a chauffeur, Job was exposed to the gardeners of the rich, and developed a love for the beauty of the Dahlia flower. Over the years, growing the flower grew into a hobby, soon Job was ordering his Dahlia flower bulbs directly from Holland in Europe. In 1953, he appeared in the *American Home Magazine*, he had won a blue ribbon from the Dahlia Society.

Job registered for the draft in 1917 and again in 1918, because World War I "the Great War" was being fought.

His next son Paul was born at South Side Hospital in Amityville on December 28, 19 ?, followed by his youngest son Harry.

Grandpa lived near the end of Brewster Lane, a small dirt road off Albany Avenue. As you neared the end of the street you came to his parent's Job and Cornelia's home, a working farm that included an orchard with apple and pear trees. By the time I reached elementary school, Uncle Kip,

Aunt Grace, and Aunt Jesse were managing the farm. The next house was my Grandpa Job's, then our house at the end of the street.

# Chapter 17

# Job(e) Valentine Brewster

Grandpa was named after his father Job(e) Valentine Brewster, who was born December 20, 1866 in North Amityville, NY. His mother was Cornelia Frances Miller born November 13, 1868 in North Amityville, N.Y. In 1915, they were living on a right-away off Albany Avenue, which later became known as Brewster Lane.

Job(e) and Cornelia had eleven children that lived, and my grandpa was the oldest:

1. Job Miller Brewster (b. July 5, 1889-90)

2. Grace M. Brewster (b. April 1891-92)

3. Hewlett J. Brewster (b. 1893-94)

4. Jessie M. Brewster (b. Nov 10, 1895)

5. Infant child Brewster (b. June 8, 1897 lived to June 11, 1897)

6. Mary Frances Brewster Steele (b. May 1899)

7. Herman Brewster (b. 1904)

8. Morgan E. Brewster (b. 1907)

9. Arlington Howard Brewster (b. May 20, 1911)

10.   Clifford "Kip" Brewster (June 16, 1912)

11.   Anita Brewster Davis (March 9, 1918)

Job(e) Valentine Brewster died on April 30, 1940 and was buried in the colored people's section of the Amityville Cemetery on May 3, 1940. I had heard that his body stayed in an upstairs bedroom for viewing by family and friends.

I remember seeing my great grandmother Cornelia in a rocking chair on her porch. She had to be over 80-years old Later, I saw her just after she passed away in one of her bedrooms. She died after World War II, and was also buried in the colored section of the cemetery. I don't remember her funeral, however their farm remained a working farm until the late 1950s.

Cornelia's parents were Jahew Miller, Jr., who was born in October 1847/1848 in Huntington (West Neck South), N.Y., and Frances R. Douglas, who was born September 8, 1854 in Rocky Point, NY near Port Jefferson. Both were of Indian ancestry!

Jahew was enumerated in Huntington (West Neck South) in the U. S. Federal Census in 1870, and 1880. In 1900 and 1920, he is enumerated living on Little Neck Road in Amityville, NY   Jahew Jr. and Frances had sixteen children:

1. Edna Miller

2. Unknown Miller

3. Unknown Miller

4. Cornelia Frances Miller (b. Nov. 13, 1868)

5. Fawn R. Miller (b. 1869)

6. Laura E. Miller (b. 1869)

7. Frederic J. Miller (b. Oct. 1873)

8. Phebe A. Miller (b. 1875)

9. Adaline Miller (b. May 28, 1876)

10. John C. Miller (b. March 1877)

11. Louis Miller (b. March 1883-85

12. Samuel Miller (b. Dec. 1884)

13. Bertha Miller (b. October 1887)

14. Catherine Miller (b. Oct. 1889)

15. Jehew (Jahew, Jehu) Miller III (b. Oct. 1892)

16. Lavina (aka Leana Miller (b. March 1896)

Jahew was the son of Jehu (Jahew) Miller, Sr., who is enumerated as a free person of color in the 1840 U. S. Federal Census, however the name of his mother is not known. I have found the names of three of their children:

1. Jehew Miller Jr. (b. Oct. 1847-48) Huntington NY

2. Lucinda Miller (b. 1854)

3. Laura E. Miller Lot (b. 1858) Rocky Point, NY

Jehu (Jahew), Sr. must have spent sometime in Rocky Point, since one of his daughters Laura E. was born in 1858 at Rocky Point.

Jahew Miller, Jr's wife Frances R. Douglas was an Indian from Rocky Point, but worked for years as a servant for the white families of Long Island. She was descent from three historic Indian clans, the Nissequogue, Setaukets, and the Unquachaugs.

The Nissequogue territory meaning Clay County was from Stony Brook to Fresh Pond, and is also said to have been from the Nissequogue River in Smithtown to Port Jefferson. This is where Chief Wyandance's mother owned land.

Frances was the daughter of James H. Douglas (b. 1824/25), and Laura Lydia Payne (b. 1834), both born in New York State.

James was a farm laborer that was enumerated in the 1860 and 1870 U. S. Federal Census living in Huntington (West Neck South), NY And in 1860, he was living next door to his daughter Frances and her husband.

I have found two (2) children for James and Laura:

1. Frances R. Douglas (b. Sept 8, 1849-1854)
2. James H. Douglas Jr. (b. 1840)

First, James Jr. married a woman named Martha _____ (b. 1850). Later, a federal census showed James married to a Laura J. Douglas (b. 1834). I believe that both Laura J. and Laura Lydia are the same person.

Laura Lydia's parents were Frances _____ (b. 1795/6), and Hannibal Payne (b. 1792-1794). Hannibal is listed in the 1860 U. S. Federal Census as "Indian." Frances and Hannibal had two (2) children:

1. Oliver Payne (b. 1820-1827)
2. Laura Lydia Payne (b. 1834)

Hannibal had also been married to an Ann _____ (b. 1802-1803), and had three (3) children in this union:

1. Margaret Payne (b. 1827-1830)
2. Black Payne (b. 1831)
3. Clark Payne (b. 1836)

Hannibal's father was Oliver Payne (b. 1772) and is listed as Indian in the 1860 U. S. Federal Census.

Both the Douglas and Payne families go back to the historic Long Island Indians, and are believed to be from the Nissequogue, Setaukets, and Unquachaugs clans.

# Chapter 18

## Job(e) A. Brewster

Job(e) Valentine Brewster's parents were Job(e) A. Brewster (b. 1835-1837) and Mary Anne Valentine (b. 1835-1837). In 1870, he is listed as a mason laborer living in the West Neck South section of Huntington.

Job (e) A. Brewster married in 1867, and was the second husband of Mary A. Valentine. Her first husband was from the Hewlett family.

Job(e) and Mary Anne had five (5) children that lived to be adults:

1. Job(e) Valentine Brewster (b. Dec 29, 1866/67)
2. Irving Brewster (b. 1868)
3. Mary E. Brewster (b. 1869)
4. Hewlett Ellsworth Brewster (b. Sept. 1874)
5. Irwin Brewster (b. 1880)

They lived on Albany Avenue and later Brewster Lane. Job(e) A. died of organic heart disease September 16, 1901.

Mary's parents were Morgan Valentine and Nancy _____. I have no further information on them.

However many of the Valentines, as well as the Hewlett family were Matinicock Natives, and slaves that were manumitted on the North shore of Long Island between 1790 and 1810. My research found a Mary, who was born to Abigail, a slave of Obediah Valentine in the Town of Oyster Bay on April 15, 1800. Prior, a Caleb Valentine was freed by Jacob Valentine in 1785, and then on October 12, 1785, he freed Massa. And on March 25, 1788, Judith was freed by Jacob Valentine.

The surname appear again during the Civil War, Charles Valentine, a 26-year old Hempstead colored man and John Valentine, a 25-year old Hempstead mulatto enlisted in the Navy.

# Chapter 19

## Charles Edgar Brewster

Job(e) A. Brewster was the child of Charles E. Brewster (b. 1809-1815) in South Oyster Bay or Huntington, N. Y, and Hannah Steele (b. 1806-1815) in Woodbury, NY

Joel Jervis, Justice of the Peace recorded on December 6, 1829 that Charles Bruster (Brewster), a colored man of Oyster Bay married Hannah Steel(e) of Huntington.

Charles and Hannah raised their thirteen (13) children in the swamps of North Amityville on the east side of Albany Avenue:

1. Sarah M. Brewster (b. 1830)

2. Martha Ann Brewster Fowler (b. 1831 – 1833)

3. John A. Brewster (b. 1835 – 1837)

4. Frances Brewster (b. 1836)

5. John Brewster (b. 1836 – 1838)

6. Lydia Brewster (b. 1839/40)

7. Charles Edgar Brewster (b. 1841/42)

8. Richard D. Brewster (b. March 1844)

9. Edward D. Brewster (b. 1845)

10. Governor Brewster (b. January 1846)

11. Sidney Brewster (b. 1850)

12. Jochavah (Jochannah) (b. 1850)

13. Hannah Brewster (b. 1889)

Charles is enumerated in the federal census of 1870 and 1880 as a farm laborer, and he died June 21, 1882 in North Amityville.

Later, Hannah Steele lived with her son Charles E. Brewster, Jr. in 1870. She was one of about six children of Charles Steele, a mulatto, and Native, who lived in the West Neck South area of Huntington.

Charles Steele's mother was a Steele, but according to Isaac Squires' will, he was Charles's father.

Isaac Squire was born when the United States was in its infancy stage between 1780 and 1790. Isaac's race is not known, but we do know that he had four (4) children including Charles by a woman named Steele. Their children were:

1. Aaron (1828)
2. Stephen (1806)
3. George (1820)
4. Charles.

Isaac had another child by a woman named Bunn:

1. Elias Bunn (about 1820-1828)

And two (2) children by a woman named Miller:

1. Samuel Miller (b. 1820 )
2. Nicholas Miller (b. 1813–1816)

However he was marry and fathered three (3) children:

1. Isaac Squires, Jr. (b. 1825–1828)
2. Daniel Squires (b. 1816–1820)
3. James Squires (b. 1805)

My research also found that there was a Charles Squires, a colored man born in 1730 - 1775 in New York, and living in the Town of Oyster Bay area of NY in 1830. He could be a relative of Isaacs.

Joel Jervis, the Justice of the Peace also married Charles' brother Elbert Bruster (Brewster) of Huntington to Anjenett Mooney of Islip on October 11, 1849. Charles Brewster and Stephen Steel(e) were witnesses.

Charles Brewster died February 16, 1887, and left a will with his brother Richard D. Brewster as executor.

about a land deed along with her Indian Tom. I have also found that an Indian killed his master, a Brewster in the Town of Brookhaven. Since slaves were property, these Indians were called Brewster's Indians, and my ancestors were the settlers' labor force.

The *Setaukets or Seatalcats'* territory stretched along the North shore from the mouth of Wading River, west to Stony Brook and Port Jefferson. The principal village was in Little Neck. And from 1655 to 1687 the Sachems were Warawakny, John Mayhew, and Gie. Members of the Mayhew family migrated to North Amityville, and can be found their today.

Around the time of the American Revolutionary War, the Indians on Long island were beginning to use surnames, and many took the surname of their white master Brewster, Valentine, Fowler, Steele, Smith, Hunter, Sells, etc.

These P-47s were equipped with wing pylons for external stores.

# Chapter 22

# From Hawaii with Love

I grew up in the shadows of my ancestors, who had lived on Long Island and those that migrated from North Carolina and Virginia. I was raised on Brewster Lane in North Amityville in their spirit; surrounded by relatives living on streets named after our family – Brewster Lane, Devine Place, Hunter Court, Steele Place, Smith Street, etc. But, there are only a few things that I remember from my very early childhood. I remember a Christmas when my father's younger brother Harry gave my sister and me gifts from Macy's in New York City.

The Christmas season was not official until Santa reached Macy's! This is where the official Santa Claus would set up shop on Thanksgiving Day and remain in residence until Christmas Eve.

It became a tradition for Phyllis and I to listen to the Macy's Thanksgiving Day Parade broadcasted on the radio, later we watched it on our 10 inch back & white television.

The Christmas Uncle Harry went shopping in New York City, our gifts were sweaters, and mine was a brown wool pullover sweater with Reindeer on it. I don't remember the design on Phyllis' sweater.

Phyllis was almost two-years older than me. She defined my early life, and I find it difficult to go on without her in the background. Phyllis died suddenly in 2000 just 3-months before her 60th birthday.

On another or the same Christmas, we received a big blue box from Hawaii. I remember Uncle Harry, Mama, Phyllis, and I opening the box. In the center of the top of our new record player was a U. S. Navy sticker. I heard this was from Bill, but I did not know who, Bill was, but had heard he was stationed in Hawaii.

Soon after I was born, my father "Bill" had enlisted in the Navy and was sent to the Chicago Great Lakes Navy Base's Camp Robert Smalls.

The U. S. Navy had begun to accept black inductees from the Selective Service Board. The new colored sailors were trained at the Great Lakes Navy Training Base, but were housed at the all-black Camp Robert Smalls' compound.

My father would become one of 167,000 blacks that served in the Navy during World War II. He would also become one of the 123,000 who served overseas.

Daddy never really talked about his Navy experience, but always had a sense of pride for being part of the war effort. I believe this was because by 1944, there was a problem of racial tension and violent outbreaks due to the Navy's segregated conditions.

Japan had attached Pearl Harbor on December 7, 1941 and Honolulu was still in shock when my father arrived on an aircraft carrier to the Pacific theatre. The sailors were placed on buses that took them to their barracks. At the first stop, all the white sailors were told to disembark, and assigned to newly built facilities. The bus continued until it reached building that should have been condemned, and the colored sailors were told to disembark. The colored sailors followed their military orders. Later the area where the colored sailors were housed was condemned by the Environmental Protection Agency (EPA) in the 1980s.

Daddy had an advantage over many of the colored sailors, since he had worked for Republic Aviation, a defense plant and a manufacturer of airplanes during the early months of the war as a aviation metal smith, after taking a 16-week training course at a vocational school.

In 1939, Republic Aviation was established when the board of directors of Seversky Aircraft ousted Alexander de Seversky as company president. They changed the name to Republic.

By the early 1940s, Republic hired many of my Long Island relatives including my father to build their planes.

With new air combat technology, Republic began planning what would turn into the P-47 Thunderbolt. The P-47 Thunderbolt was ranked as one of the three best fighters of World War II along with Lockheed's P-38 Lightning and North American's P-51 Mustang.

Republic built 773 of the P-47 planes in Farmingdale near North Amityville, but production of the P-47 ended in November 1945 with the war.

From the Great Lakes, Daddy was deployed to a base in California, and then assigned to an aircraft carrier. Onboard the aircraft carrier, most of the colored sailors were cooks or cleaned the carrier, spending most of their time below deck. But my Daddy serviced the planes on the deck, as well as where they were stored below deck.

I'm not sure which aircraft carrier Daddy served on, but the largest carriers were capable of launching over 90 aircraft.

During World War II, most small aircraft were usually stored below the deck and taken to the landing strip by the aircraft carrier elevators. Because the strip was short, a catapult (usually a piston-type device driven by steam from the ship's boilers) helped launch the aircraft into the air. Planes landing on the carriers used a hook on the bottom of the plane to catch a wire, strung across the deck, which helped bring the plane to a complete stop.

A central control tower was located to the side of the landing strip and housed advanced radio and radar equipment used to keep in touch with pilot.

The *HMS Ark Royal* circa early 1939.

Daddy was discharged from service a few months after the war ended, and received the: American Theatre, Asiatic Pacific and Victory medals.

Later, I learned that my relatives had fought in the Indian wars, American Revolution, War of 1812, Spanish American War, World War I, and now World War II. Young men like my father Bill had left their wife and children behind to go to fight for what they believed.

Relatives like my uncle Harry, who were too young to enlist were left to help the family at home until their brothers and fathers returned from war.

# Chapter 23

# My Uncle Harry

My Uncle Harry was my father's youngest brother and the baby of five children, and my mother would always add "the change of life baby." However, it was not unusual for women to have babies late in their 40s just before their change of life.

Harry was only about thirteen when my parents married and fifteen when his mother died, the year I was born. It's sad, but my Uncle Harry was murdered February 14, 1952.

I remember his principal Mr. Dayton would come in the morning and pick him up for school or was he the triune officer. My mother also had explained to me, "Triune officers picked bad children up and took them to school." They had them in those years, because the New York State Education Department paid school district for the children that actually attended school.

Mr. Dayton, a white man would stand at the foot of my grandfather's stairs at 63 Brewster Lane and call for Uncle Harry. "Harry, you have to go to school." His voice would go pass our Singer sewing machine where my cat "Blackie" would hide underneath the treadle, then the sound floated up the stairs towards Uncle Harry's room.

Buster, my late grandmother Catherine's Bull dog would stand next to my mother and listen for movement.

Buster had a reputation in North Amityville for killing chickens and fighting with other dogs. In a fight a couple years later, he grabbed hold of another dog and held onto him all afternoon. The two dogs fought out-and-inside my grandfather's house until Wilda went up to Republic Aviation and got Bill from work. This must have happened around 1946, when Republic was designing their XF-91 Thunderceptor. It was America's first combat-type fighter to fly faster than the speed of sound. Daddy was home from the Navy, and was working in the Experimental Department.

Buster lived for years, however I really do not know what happened to him, but Phyllis and I were told he went away to die.

"Harry" making a left turn, the sound would go pass Phyllis' room on the right. Her room was small and overlooked my Grandfather's backyard, his overgrown with weeds vegetable garden, and his empty gold fishpond. You could also see an outhouse on Devine Place from her bed near one of the two windows. But before you reached the outhouse stood one surviving gravestone in the Brewster Indian cemetery behind grandpa's house.

Across the hall from Phyllis' room, my mother and my room sat on the front of the house. We also had two windows. Grandpa's house was a three-bedroom house with a center hall. My mother always kept a slop pot under her bed. I learned in later years that the house had been built without its one bathroom, which was added to the back of the house, as well as without electricity which was added later.

Before living at Grandpa's house, my parents had rented a room on Albany Avenue at Mr. Taylor's home. My mother's cousin Sonny and his wife Otis also lived there.

Again Mr. Dayton called, "Harry, I'm waiting." The sound traveled until it hit the door of a small dark room with a bed under its only window, and a dresser. There were a lot of wires and unfinished projects, as well as experiments hidden in this private space. Some of which Phyllis and I had been the willing subjects, as well as the target. Most were developed to protect a teenager's privacy from his young nieces. There were also parts of a crystal radio left by his older brothers.

Harry rallied and would go off to public school with this white man Mr. Dayton. By the time I entered elementary school, Mr. Dayton had become a principal.

# Chapter 24

## Uncle Harry Told Me Too!

My sister Phyllis was always old and responsible! When mama shopped in the village at the A & P supermarket, Uncle Harry would have to take time from hanging out with his friends at Uncle Hewlett's poolroom and watch me.

Uncle Hewlett was one of my grandfather Job's brother.

However, I liked going to the other side of the Long Island railroad tracks to the A & P and across the street to the Johnson Meat Market because the butchers would always reach over the counter and hand me a fresh slice of a cold cuts.

The Atlantic & Pacific Tea Company (A & P Supermarket) owners George Huntington Hartford and George Gilman had established the supermarkets in 1859 throughout North America; however I don't know when the one was built in the village.

On a shopping trip, when I did not go with Mama and Phyllis, Uncle Harry was told to watch me. He placed me upstairs on the side of my mother's bed, and told me not to move giving me a box of Vicks Cough Drops then instructing me to eat one at a time.

Vicks Cough Drops were menthol flavored, since cherry flavoring was not introduced until after the Korean War. The Vick Chemical Company began marketing the menthol cough drops in 1931 with instant success. Despite the stock market crash of 1929 and the economic chaos that followed Americans still caught colds.

Uncle Harry left me alone with my cough drops, and went to the small wood building, which housed Uncle Hewlett's poolroom at the beginning of Brewster Lane.

Most of my Uncle Harry's friends at poolroom were relatives, and Uncle Hewlett kept them from getting into trouble. He cashed checks, loaned money, counseled on marriage affairs, and listened to problems.

I followed Uncle Harry's instructions eating one cough drop at a time until my mother came home, and found me sitting there. When she questioned me, I told her "Uncle Harry told me too." Uncle Harry was never left to watch me again, and I got to go to the A & P and Johnson's Meat Market to get the fresh cold cut slices.

I attended public school with Mr. Johnson's son Danny, years later, I taught in Middletown, NY, where Danny was the gym teacher.

# Chapter 25

# L. I. Railroad Family Day

When Uncle Harry got out of high school, his first job was working for the Long Island Railroad, but I don't know what he did at work. I assume it was on the assemble line where they repaired and cleaned the trains.

The Long Island Railroad was chartered on April 24, 1834; it is the oldest railroad still operating in the U. S.

During Uncle Harry's brief employment, Phyllis and I would get to attend Family Day in Long Island City, and go through the round house where the trains were turned around. The trains would head out again for all points east until they reached Bayshore. Here they paused out of guilt, before venturing towards Montauk Point through the land the Long Island Railroad took from the Montauk and Shinnecock Indians.

My Grandpa Brewster looked like an Indian straight off the reservation with his black hair and high cheekbones. He had moved to a small walk-up apartment in Brooklyn after my Grandmother Catherine's death. We never went to New York City with Mama until Bill came home from Hawaii. And that was because Grandpa Jobe had got married to

Gladys Underhill, a city widow woman, who had two daughters Helen and Eva.

Grandpa's 2nd wife Gladys was showing an interest in Harry, Phyllis and me by taking us on this journey to the Long Island Railroad Family Day.

Gladys grew up in Redding, Pennsylvania, and had gone to school with the famous Paul Robeson, an actor, athlete, attorney, and singer, best known for "Ol' Man River." Her first husband's family was freedmen from Oklahoma City, Oklahoma. Her sister Helen was an art teacher and poet in Philadelphia Public School System and her brother Dr. Underhill was a missionary in Africa.

Mama did not go to Family Day, since it was always an ordeal for her to go anywhere besides the village, and she might have been pregnant with my brother. But most of the colored people in North Amityville didn't travel more than 30-minutes from their home, and my mother was no different.

Most of Grandpa's brother were working or had worked for the Long Island Railroad. I remember seeing Uncle Morgan working in the upholstery shop, along with Uncle Charlie Steele, who was married to Aunt Maime, Grandpa's sisters.

Did the Long Island Railroad hire these non-reservation Indians (Steele, Brewster, Douglas) out of guilt?

Our car looked like this!

Source: www.nashcarclub.org

# Chapter 26

# Our Nash

My father Bill purchased for my mother Wilda, a woman in her twenties a convertible blue Nash with a standard shift car before leaving for the Navy. According to Wilda, the car sometime worked and sometime did not. I think gas and oil rationing during the war were the main problems, but Wilda would not let anyone touch Bill's car.

Wilda never understood anything mechanical, and always had trouble driving. In fact, Phyllis and I went with her to the motor vehicle office in Bayshore to take her driver's test. She drove the car onto the sidewalk and could not parallel park! It was a bad experience for a small child; however the tester gave Wilda, a driver's license because Bill was in the armed service fighting to make the world safe for democracy.

After World War II, Mama would be showing off Amityville Village to Grandpa Jobe's new wife Gladys, and stall the Nash on the railroad tracks, the racial dividing line between the two Amityville communities.

The gate man came out of his little building shouting at my mother. "Move your car!" He was upset that this colored woman would not move her car.

The train engineer blew his whistle and the steam engine puffed dark smoke. He was building up power to take the train to Copiague, Babylon, Lindenhurst and Bayshore. He leaned out the side window of the engine shouting "move your car" as he checked his watch. He had a schedule to keep! The engineer was not going to let this colored person get him off schedule.

Sitting in the back seat with my sister Phyllis, I was frightened as the Nash's engine grinned trying its best to start. Alarmed, Phyllis took my hand and was about to get out of the car taking me to safety, when another driver's car pushed us off the railroad tracks. On the other side, the Nash finally started, and my shaken mother drove full throttle to the safety of the North Amityville community on the "colored" side of the railroad tracks.

Our home looked very much like this!

# Chapter 27

## Our Cape Cod Style Home

Soon after Bill came home from the Navy, he began to build our Cape Cod house at the end of Brewster Lane. When he cleared the land, an Indian arrowhead was found. He gave it to Phyllis, who kept it for years.

Daddy worked nights at Republic Aviation again, and all of his free time was spent on building our home. Phyllis even helped to nail some two-by-fours. I was too young, and really did not know Bill, so I stayed close to my mother.

After we moved into the house, Daddy and Mama waited awhile to have my brother Hodgie. I think their biggest problem was I had spent the first few years of my life sharing a bedroom with my mother. And now I had to share a room with my sister and sleep in my own twin bed. Every night I went to sleep in my parent's bed, and later was taken to my bedroom. We didn't have rationing books, so life was different after the war at our new house.

On Thursday Dugan "the bread man" would deliver our bread and cup cakes with chocolate sugar frosting. For awhile, we had the soda man delivering cases of soda, but that did not last long.

Mr. Roper, who had a dairy farm on Harrison Avenue, delivered our milk to a metal box on our front porch. The cream in the unpasteurized bottle of milk would rise to the top, because it came straight from his cows. He was one of the immigrants that didn't move away from our community.

One day, his bull got loose and terrorized the children in our neighborhood. Phyllis and I ran home from Smith Street, and to distract the bull she throw my red sweater onto our front lawn. Later, Mr. Roper caught his bull and took him back to the pasture on Harrison Avenue.

I don't remember who the ice man was, but the ice was delivered in a big chunk that was placed in the freezer of our icebox. The ice kept our food cold until Mama needed it for cooking. By the time my brother was born, we had graduated to a new GE electric refrigerator with a freezer.

In the winter, the coal man, who was located near the Powell's Moving Company behind the A & P Supermarket in the village would deliver black coal. Phyllis and I would run to the basement to watch it being dumped into our coal bin. But when we lived in Grandpa's house during the war, sometimes Mama couldn't get coal, so she would burn our wooden toys and chairs in the furnace.

Around the time my brother was a baby, Daddy installed a central heating system. This was located in the center of our house. We could effort the modern system, Daddy was working days in his J & W Mason Contractor business and nights at Republic Aviation, so we were on "easy" street.

And once a week the insurance man collected one or two dollar for our life insurance policies. These were the white people that serviced the families of North Amityville.

The hamlet of North Amityville had a few colored entrepreneurs like Daddy that supplied some of the other needed services. On Albany Avenue there was Jimmy, the barber and further down the street was Brown's store, where you could buy groceries or play the numbers. And for awhile, Aunt Jenny and Uncle Morgan had a grocery store, also on Albany Avenue. Louis Leftenant picked up our garbage and his brother Chris would clean your cesspool. If you drove towards the Village of Amityville on Albany Avenue, you would have to pass Uncle Bill Davis' gas station. The first colored doctor in town was Dr. Jones, who had an office on Broadway. And then there was Freddie's Rendezvous, the local juke joint on Albany Avenue.

Daddy Bill and his cousin Jim started J & W Mason Contractors. The "W" was for Willis, Daddy's real name. At the prime of their business, they had three or four trucks, cement mixers, etc. Some of their projects were in

Lindenhurst or Copiague; they built the Wise Potato Chip factory, and a furniture store on Merrick Road in Amityville. For Levitt that built the original Levittown, they laid the slab of cement that the white veteran houses were built on. There were many more projects that made them a success.

Leftenant, Davis, and Brewster were young business men ahead of their times, there was no Small Business Administration (SBA), and local banks would not give colored men business loans or checking accounts. I remember on Thursday night, Phyllis and I would help Daddy stuff cash into small brown pay envelopes for his Friday payroll.

Other services we received indirectly from the Town of Babylon because Uncle Kip and some of our Devine cousins worked for the town. They would make sure we got plowed during a snow storm; since Brewster Lane was considered just a right-away.

# Chapter 28

# Phyllis' Cinderella Watch

As I mentioned Phyllis was the oldest child in the house, and she spent most of her time with my mother, Cousin Margie or her friend Carolyn Green.

The Greens lived just across the "big lot" that separated Brewster Lane and Smith Street in front of grandpa's house.

One year for her birthday, Phyllis got a new Cinderella watch that glowed in the dark from our parents. She convinced Caroline and me to go into our bedroom closet to see the watch glow. We closed the door and the hands on watch dial glowed bright. But when we went to open the door the knob just turned, and didn't open. We were locked in a dark closet, and our only light was the watch that glowed.

Phyllis knew I was scared of the dark, so she told me to just keep looking at the watch. "Sandra, you are the shortest, so you take the bottom air," Phyllis told me. She gave Caroline the middle air, and since she was the tallest, Phyllis took the upper air. But we were comforted by the glow of the watch!

We were in the closet for sometime, but finally Mama came inside the house from hanging up sheets on our clothes line. We yelled, screamed and banged on the door until she open it. Carolyn was sent home, Phyllis and I were punished, but I still wanted to have a watch like my sister's that glowed in the dark.

Two people in North Amityville worked for the federal government and were like the watch that glowed in the dark, Carolyn's father Tommy Green worked for the U. S. Post Office and my Godfather Robert Bean worked for the Internal Revenue Service.

Robert Cyril Bean's parents Maude L. and Ralph Freeman Bean were originally from Bermuda. But Uncle Robert grew up in Amityville with my parents, and attended Amityville Public Schools. Following his graduation was drafted into the U.S. Army and served as a sergeant in the South Pacific at Luzon, New Guinea and the Southern Philippines. He received the Asiatic Pacific Service Medal, the Philippines Liberation Ribbon, and Victory Medal. After the war, he worked for the federal government's Internal Revenue Service (IRS), then as a clerk in Grand Central Railroad Terminal in New York City.

He never missed giving me a birthday or a holiday gift, however while working with the IRS he met his future wife

Eliza Jane _____. The couple was married in June, 1948 and my gifts got fewer and fewer as their four children were born. Uncle Robert stayed active in the community as a trustee on the Board of Directors of the North Amityville Taxpayers Association, and was a commander from 1969 – 1970 of the Hunter Squire Jackson Post 1218.

Tommy Green was also a commander of the Hunter-Squire-Jackson Legion Post 1218. However Uncle Robert died February 17, 2001 at 79 years old.

Tommy Green and Robert Bean had a real commitment to the North Amityville community that is worth recognizing.

Powell's Moving Company
Source: www.amityvillehistoricalsociety.org

# Chapter 29

# The Path

My cousin Margie lived on Albany Avenue with her brother Donald and their parents Otis Travis born in Virginia, and Donald "Sonny" Edward Broadnick. She was like Phyllis "perfect," and her pants never dropped like mine.

During World War II, when my mother was trying to train me to use the bathroom, she had to use "pre-owned" panties without elastic. Most of my clothes were pre-owned except for the holiday outfits. There was a World War being fought and elastic was not available, so safety pins were used. Regardless my family still nicknamed me "droppy draws."

Besides the problem with elastic, the Federal government rationed food, gas and clothing. Mama would receive war rationing books based on our small family size. Everyone was sacrificing; however the coupons didn't mean that the items would be available. And to complicate the matter, the stamps also had an expiration date.

*Red ration stamps* allowed Mama to buy a certain amount of meats, butter, fats, oils and cheese from the A & P supermarket and Johnson's Meat Market.

War Ration Books & Stamps

*Blue ration stamps* covered our canned goods, bottled items, fruits, vegetables, juices, dry beans, processed food, soups, baby foods and catsup.

There were *gas and tire rationing stamps* for Bill's car, but Mama didn't get many of these stamps.

In May 1943, sugar rationing went into effect with the distribution of a *sugar buying card*, so candy was a real treat.

If, you ran out of ration stamps, families could try to buy more illegally for a higher price on the Black Market. But to help feed the children, most colored families started *victory gardens*! From their victory gardens Otis, Aunt Maime, Aunt Grace, Aunt Jesse, and Mrs. Hunter like most women canned vegetables and fruit.

While, we lived at Grandpa's house Phyllis would hold my hand and we would walk from our backyard over to Devine Place, then down the path of Sonny and Otis' garden. We would pass the vegetables, and then the lilacs flowers, grapevines, and run pass their outhouse. We entered the backdoor and would be given homemade ice cream at the kitchen table. I wanted to be like Phyllis and Margie able to take this trip without having my hand held.

For years Margie would always produce special events for the older children like Phyllis. My mother, Aunt Lil, and Otis would be the audience for the performances and the little children like me were considered the uninvited guest.

Her father Sonny worked for Powell's Moving Company just behind the A & P. But, he would disappear for a period of time, perhaps a week or two. Upon returning home, he would bring back large citrus fruits that were a cross between oranges and tangerines from a place called Florida. Children were seen and not heard, but I heard the adults talking about Sonny and the railroad.

Sonny also worked as a Pullman porter for the Southern Atlantic-Pacific Railroad, and was a member of the Brotherhood of Sleeping Car Porters (BSCP) founded by A. Philip Randolph in 1925. By the 1920s over 20,224 colored men were working as Pullman porters, and were known as a man called *George*.

The BSCP union forced the Pullman Company to the bargaining table, and after 12-years on August 25, 1937 were recognized as the official porters union. The Pullman Company porters were "ambassadors of hospitality," according to the A. Philip Randolph Pullman Porter Museum in Chicago, IL.

Later, I would take the same path a little further pass Otis and Sonny's backyard to Hunter Court, where Christine and Carol Hunter lived with their father Robert H. Hunter, a son of Milford Hunter and Hannah E. Fowler. And their mother Geraldine Webster Mills was the daughter of Frances Mills of Huntington.

The big house where the Hunter family lived at the dead end of the street was owned by David Fowler, a brother of Hannah and my great-grandfather Royal.

Christine's older sister June attended Hunter College in New York City, and after graduating became the first colored teacher in the Amityville public school system.

Many years before the district had been segregated, the colored teachers taught in the small one room Colored Huntington School District Building #6 on Albany Avenue near Sunrise Highway.

Walking from the Hunter's home, we would come to Uncle Bob's house on the left. Robert Scurlock was my Grandpa Scurlock's brother.

Grandma Scurlock's brother Frederick and Uncle Bob had been soldiers in the famous colored 369th regiment during World War I. Along with others Uncle Bob's names were placed on the big clock at the Amityville Triangle in the Village.

After the war my Grandma Scurlock along with thousands of people attended the parade when the 369th soldiers came home from France and proudly marched up 125th Street in Harlem, New York City.

Source: National Archives and Record Administration,
Records of the War Department, Record Group 165, Identifier 533553

Continuing down Hunter Court to Albany Avenue, if you took a right-turn passed Uncle Bill and Aunt Anita Davis' gas station, you could walk to the Village, but a left-turn took us back to Sonny's house.

Besides the moving company where Sonny worked the Powell family owned a small funeral home directly across from the A & P supermarket and next door to the Johnson Meat Market.

One day after going to Uncle Bob's house and seeing him lying still, I would sit in the small Powell's Funeral Home in the front row with Phyllis and Margie. Uncle Bob would be in a box looking gray, and I was too young to know what was happening. The music was spooky, the adults were crying and I was frightened. Uncle Bob's was the first funeral I attended, but we would return to this building when Grandpa Scurlock died.

Near the funeral home was Fred Smith's Taxi Cab, the only "colored" business in the village. They had an office and waiting room with a potbelly stove to keep the colored people warm in the winter, as they waited for a car to return and take them to the safety of the North Amityville hamlet.

The adults talked about the Smith family being from Shinnecock and Huntington, as well as being our relatives, but now they lived in Copiague. The older children came to the village to drive the cabs with their parents. And Fred's daughter Rena took Christine Hunter and me to kindergarten each day.

The path connected colored families starting near Ernest Hunter's backyard and his outhouse, cut across Brewster Lane, Devine Place, the Broadnick's yard, Hunter Court, and then ended at Sunrise Highway.

World War II Unit – Village of Amityville web site

Source: www.amityville.org

# Chapter 30

# The Amityville Parade

Broadway would cross the Long Island Railroad train tracks heading towards North Amityville. When a train would start to leave the Amityville train station, the gate man would come out of his little building, and would turn a handle that lowering the gates. And he would hope that women like my mother Wilda were not stuck on the railroad tracks.

The train with its steam engine would be blowing smoke and sounding a whistle as it approached Broadway. Again the train engineer would look to make sure the tracks were clear, so he could keep his schedule. But on Memorial Day, the Amityville parades would start in the village and cross the railroad tracks taking the left road up Broadway pass the white families to Harrison Avenue.

Just after World War II, Uncle Junior, Uncle Robert, Tommy Green and my Daddy would march with the other veterans, and later Phyllis would march with her Brownie troop in the Amityville parade to the Amityville Cemetery on Harrison Avenue.

This early parades saluted the veterans as far back as the Civil War. Being driven in a car, I remember seeing a relative Governor Brewster, who had been in the 26th United State Colored Troop (USCT).

The cemetery was the largest in the area, but there were small Indian and colored cemeteries in North Amityville too. Just off Bethpage Road, there was a Brewster cemetery and another Brewster/Steele cemetery behind my grandfather's house on Brewster Lane. The Bunn family also had their cemetery off Bethpage Road. The Squire cemetery was off Great Neck Road between Johnson Street and Columbus Blvd. And the Fowler cemetery was just off Bayview Avenue. But as the community grew the colored families began to bury their relatives in the Amityville Cemetery.

The official parade would end on the front lawn of the white section of the cemetery. Once dressed in his Navy uniform Daddy was in the color guard, when the guns fired their salute, I thought they had shot Bill and began to scream. Comforting me, my mother took me to the safety of the colored section behind the trees and pauper's field in the back of the cemetery, Pauper's field was where infants that died at birth, unidentified bodies, and the very poor were buried.

The Amityville cemetery was segregated, and the colored graves were hidden from view of the Village of Amityville residents.

After driving or walking down the dirt road to the back of the cemetery the unofficial colored community parade would begin. The colored parade was led by the Hunter-Squires-Jackson American Legion Post – 1218's Drum and Bugle Corp. that marched in high step and rhythm to the small legion hall building next to Freddie's Rendezvous, the local colored juke joint.

The lead majorette was Vivian, Grandma Scurlock's brother Fred's daughter, and Aunt Irma also marched with the early Drum and Bugle Corp.

Across the street from Freddie's Rendezvous was a dirt road that led to two large houses surround by dirt not grass where Royal Fowler, my Grandma Scurlock's father once lived.

Most of the members of the colored parade were my relatives the Hunters, Millers, Squires, Steeles, Devines, and Brewsters.

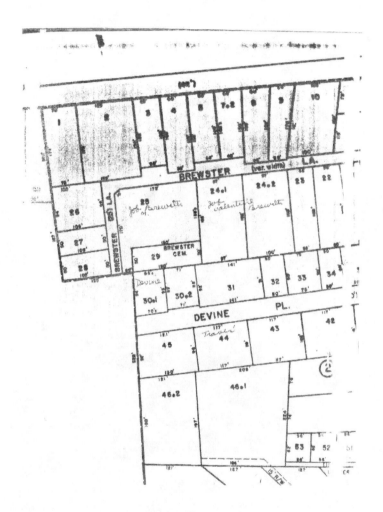

Brewster Cemetery

Edgar A. Scurlock, Jr. – January 9, 1943 –
Camp Pickett< VA – Quarter Master

# Chapter 31

## Mama's Sister & Brother

I don't remember my mother's parents ever living together. Grandpa Scurlock lived a number of places, which we never visited. We saw him mostly at Aunt Lil or Cousin Sonny's houses, but always on one of his many visits to our home. He died November 10, 1951. Grandpa Scurlock died November 10, 1951 and he never got to see my youngest sister.

I don't know what Grandpa Scurlock did for a living besides being a chauffeur or anything else about his life. Recently, I found out that he had a daughter Clarisse out of wedlock before getting married. She lived around Hempstead, but later moved to Boston, Massachusetts were she died.

How my grandparents met and were married is a mystery to me. My grandparents really didn't live together together, but I have an idea why. Grandma Scurlock worked as a live-in domestic, and Grandpa Scurlock worked as a live-in chauffeur. Most of the time, they worked for different families.

My mother's sister was Mary Irma; she was also my God mother. I loved Aunt Irma like a big sister. She was beautiful and a really cool person with the nicest clothes. For hours, I would sit and watch her select an outfit from her closet.

About a year before Grandpa Scurlock died Aunt Irma married Charles "Buddy" Miller. His Millers were not related to us, thank God! They were some of the new colored people in North Amityville.

Uncle Buddy remained one of the nicest people I ever new. He was kind, quite and a very hard worker. He worked all of his life repairing shoes in the Amityville Village shoe shop next to the 5 & 10 cent store. Their marriage lasted a few years in which they bought a house in the Roneck Park development that was built for colored GIs in North Amityville.

My mother's brother was Uncle Junior or Edgar A. Scurlock, Jr. Like Bill, Uncle Junior had served in World War II, but in the U. S. Army. First, he was stationed at Camp Pickett, Virginia, then Calcutta, India. My cousin Ernest Hunter, Jr., son of Ernest Hunter Sr. and Katherine Sinclair Hunter was also in the Army in Calcutta, but died there during the war. In North Amityville, Katherine became a Gold Star Mother along with Eunice Middleton Leftenant.

The flight officer Samuel Leftenant was a son of Eunice and James Leftenant, Sr., originally of South Carolina, a member of the Tuskegee Airman Class of 1944 and died when his plane was lost over Europe during the war.

*Gold Star Mothers* is a term that came into general use in 1928 with the creation of the service flag given to families that's daughter or son died in the U. S. Armed Service. It's best described by a proclamation of the President approved June 23, 1936 (Public Resolution 123, 74th Congress) that stated:

*"Whereas the American Gold Star Mothers suffered the supreme sacrifice of motherhood in the loss of their sons and daughters in World Wars"*

Towards the end of the war, Uncle Junior married Mercy, an East Indian woman and had a son Edgar Aaron Scurlock, III. It took over eighteen years for the American Red Cross and the U. S. Army to arranged for him to join his father in the United States, but by then Little Edgar had no interest in coming to America.

After the war, Uncle Junior would work driving a dump truck for my father's business, when he was not working as a chauffer for a white family.

Uncle Junior's 2nd wife was Justine Johnson, a beautiful woman from Brooklyn New York. While they were married, I named all of my dolls after Aunt Justine. But most of the time Uncle Junior lived at the home of Grandma Scurlock.

# Chapter 32

# The Great Depression 1929 - 1939

The stock market crashed in October 1929 changing my parent's world. They were both in Amityville Public Elementary School, and were being filled up at dinner on homemade baked bread. When there wasn't enough food, the adults gave the children a lot of bake bread, so they would not go hungry, my mother told me.

By 1932 approximately one out of every four Americans was unemployed. The white families that had hired chauffeurs and domestics could no longer pay them.

How colored people suffered during the Great Depression is linked to racial discrimination. They had been the "last hired and first fired." They became jobless in disproportionate numbers. Colored unemployment was also aided by the racist attitude that whites should not be without work, while colored people were employed. Whites began to apply for traditional colored jobs as domestics, porters, elevator operators, trash collectors, and chauffeurs. And bread lines became common even on Long Island.

My mother was being raised by her grandparents and aunts, while her parents worked miles away for different white families to try to survive.

In 1933 the new president, Franklin Roosevelt quickly rallied America to a new program known as the New Deal. "The only thing we have to fear is fear itself," Roosevelt declared in his inaugural address. President Roosevelt backed a new set of economic and social measures that would even help my grandparents.

The Works Progress Administration (WPA), the principal relief agency of the so-called second New Deal was attempting to provide work rather than welfare. Under the WPA, buildings, roads, airports and schools were constructed. Actors, painters, musicians and writers were employed through the Federal Theater Project, the Federal Art Project and the Federal Writers Project. In addition, the National Youth Administration gave part-time employment to students; established training programs provided aid to unemployed youth. But the New Deal's cornerstone, according to Roosevelt was the Social Security Act of 1935.

The Great Depression reduced employment opportunities in the North for colored people causing the migration to slow.

Traditional colored churches were providing food, clothing, and housing for the needy. In addition the Nation of Islam, the United House of Prayer of All People of Daddy Grace, and the Kingdom of Peace Movement of Father Divine offered free inexpensive meals and lodgings.

My mother said, she will never forget being young during the Depression years, and would always place a stack of bread on our dinner table.

# Chapter 33

## Ocean Avenue

My Grandmother Scurlock finally got the opportunity to work as a live-in domestic in the Village of Amityville during the late 1940s for the O'Keefe family. As a live-in she returned to colored community for just 2-days a week.

Grandma Scurlock would live at Cousin Bert's house on the corner of Great Neck Road and Sunrise Highway where she had a room in the front and kept her slop pot in the closet, and then her house on Sunrise Highway, both in Copiague, NY, and finally her house at 28 Coolidge Avenue in Amityville.

Cousin Bertha or Bert was born 1885 in New York State, and later married Frank Aldridge, an engineer, who worked in the city. Her parents were James Coster (b. 1868) and Martha Green Fowler (b. 1866). James was a dentist, who made false teeth. Martha's mother was a Green and her father was George W. Fowler (b. 1837-1841), the brother of Grandma Scurlock's father Royal. Martha spent her final years at her house on Albany Avenue just south of Sunrise Highway, after her death Cousin Bert moved into her house.

Grandma saved her money and purchased a model home from a builder next door to Cousin Bert's house in Copiague, soon after she had to sell it, since New York State was widening Sunrise Highway. The state was taking the colored people's property under the eminent domain laws.

Cousin Bert's house was sold and moved down on Simmons Street, and Grandma brought a house on Coolidge Avenue at the end where the white immigrants had lived just across the street from Lou Howard's parents.

Lou Howard was a high school teacher, football coach, mayor, and then a NY State Legislator.

However since the 1940s, Grandma had lived at the O'Keefe on Ocean Avenue, where she cooked and cleaned until retiring as a live-in domestic.

The O'Keefe's house was in South Amityville on the other side of the village on the canals near the Amityville Beach.

Mama, Phyllis and I would pick Grandma up from Ocean Ave. on Thursday afternoon along with the Lady Fingers cookies that her boss would send to us children. As a child, I thought the O'Keefes were relatives, even though we never entered the front door. I didn't think this was strange, since we entered most houses through the back or side doors.

At the O'Keefe's home, we were allowed to play near the canal and the Great South Bay even when the white family was in residence.

On most occasions we waited in the car or the kitchen for Grandma. My mother would help her bring clothing and other items in brown bags to our car. Grandma would leave her domestic life and the white world of the Village behind for a few days.

While home, she would take an active part in the colored community, she would be active in the women's auxiliary of the colored Hunter-Squires-Jackson American Legion Post because her brother was the Jackson in the legions' name. She became president of the auxiliary on a number of occasions. Later, she was very active in the Bethel AME Church in North Amityville.

Every Sunday, Grandma would be in church with her white gloves, hat, and mink stole that Mrs. O'Keefe had given her.

For a couple of days, we actually got to play on Ocean Avenue, Mama and her sister Irma were asked by their mother to clean a neighbor of Mrs O'Keefe's house. Phyllis and I got to play throughout the house. I think they were getting the house ready for the white family to return from that place called Florida.

Grandma was beautiful and looked like she had just left the Indian reservation, but she was considered an "off-reservation" Indian. She kept her hair in a bun, but on occasions we would catch a glimpse of how it would hang long past her waist. With her high cheekbones, and long hair no one could dispute her Indian heritage.

OLD A. M. E. CHURCH, ERECTED 1844

# Chapter 34

# Spiritual Seeker

Our family attended the original Bethel AME Church erected in 1844 on Albany Avenue near the Purdy farm.

During the years between 1814-1839 colored families in North Amityville like Squires, Payne, Hunter, Brewster, Steele and Miller held Sunday school meetings and religious services in their homes. The small religious group was in need of a church building, so in 1839 Elias Hunter deeded land near the Squires and Payne family on Albany Avenue.

One hundred and five years later, I attended Sunday school in the church home built in 1844 on the Hunter property. However, we also participated in the events held at the Baptist Church on the corner of Albany Ave and Steele Place. This church would always have a Tom Thumb Wedding, and if I remember it correctly I was in two of them. I was never the bride, always a flower girl.

The real "General" Tom Thumb was Charles Stratton, a midget from Connecticut, who became an entertainer with the Ringling Brothers Barnum and Bailey Circus at the age of four. In 1863, Stratton married Lavinia Warren also a dwarf in a highly publicized and lavish wedding.

The public adored the spectacle, so much that a play based on the couple's wedding was developed. Community groups began performing "Tom Thumb Wedding" throughout the country, casting young children in the roles of Mr. and Mrs. Tom Thumb. Later, the play was developed into a fundraiser for local churches

I don't remember how we got involved in the event or who produced the event, but Phyllis and I would go to practice every week.

One of the mothers on Smith Street made all of our dresses, and my cousins the Millers, Hunters, Caldwells, Devines and other Brewsters were in the weddings. I enjoyed the production; however the adults that worked really hard on the event never told us the history of Tom Thumb.

Back at Bethel AME Church, Phyllis and I would attend Sunday school. I think this was around the time that my brother Hodgie was born, since I don't remember my other sisters being in the picture.

Mama would "grease us up" with Vaseline smearing and polishing it on our faces, arms, legs and hair. Later, I learned from Grandpa that this was an Indian custom; greasing children in the summer protected them from the sun, whereas in the winter it protected them against the cold chilly Long Island air.

The Bethel AME Church's parsonage was where Phyllis was being christened when Pearl Harbor was attacked, but I was christened in the church after Bill came home from the war.

By the time Phyllis and I could go to Sunday school by ourselves, we had moved down the hill to 69 Brewster Lane. We would walk up the hill past Grandpa Job's house, and then continue down Brewster Lane to Albany Ave. We would go left past Mrs Franklin's house, Brown's Deli until we got to Uncle Morg and Aunt Jennie's grocery store.

Sometime, we would spend part of our Sunday school money before we went to church, and sometime after. But Uncle Morg and Aunt Jennie would always give us extra penny candy. Uncle Morg was my grandpa Job's brother, and he was one of my uncles that worked on the Long Island Railroad.

At Sunday school Phyllis was in the class with the older children and I was in the little children's class. I was shy and could not read well, because the words were fuzzy! I needed glasses! And hated when my Sunday School teacher would call on me.

The little children's class would sit in pews in the back of the church, and the teacher would sit in a row in front of us and look over the seat.

The words were always fussy like in school, even if I could see them I couldn't sound them out. The New York State Board of Education was trying a new system to teach children to read by sight. And I was being taught in the first grade to recognize the words. Once I saw a word, I remembered what it meant and sounded like. And then again, the *Jim and Judy* reading book in school did not keep my attention. They were mostly about little white children getting a new red wagon. I could not relate to our public school reading books, but did not know why.

Sunday school was a mystery to me! I never understood most of the bible, as well as how it fit into my life. I colored the pictures that were given to me, and even remembered some of the stories. But never understood why I was there! Some of the children seemed to get it, and were always the center of attention.

After Sunday school before continuing down the hill to our house, Phyllis and I would stop at Grandpa Brewster's houses.

Week after week, Grandpa would show us the same pictures and tell us the same oral history stories. Finally he would either get board with us or feel his job was finished, and then give us $1.00 each for the movies. This was a lot of money, since the movies was $0.25.

This ritual took place on Grandpa's porch, or in his living room next to the secretariat desk that had the ivory carved elephant tusk, which Dr. Underhill had brought back from Africa.

Grandma Gladys would give us a glass of Kool Aide to drink and we would hear about Yamaqua, who walked from the Indian land down east to Amityville. Grandpa would tell us about going to Detroit to learn to fix his boss' car and his trip to Europe as a chauffer. The Sunday ritual lasted throughout my early church years.

One Christmas Phyllis and I had verses to remember for the Christmas program at our church. I was excited, since I would get a new red dress.

Every year Mama would always buy me a red velvet dress with Mary Jane black patten leather shoes from Lang's shoe store in the village. On a few occasions the dress would be file and not velvet, but always red. It was exciting, since we would travel away from our community and the village to shop in Hempstead, Freeport, or Bayshore.

My Cousin Marjorie helped me memorize my verse. I had my red dress, black patten leather shoes, and was ready.

On the night of the performance, the children entered the church through the basement, and waited there until we were called upstairs to say our verse. When I got upstairs I was scared, however I could see Marjorie on my right side in a pew mouthing the words. I looked directly at her and repeated what she said. I ended my verse that evening with "Is that right Marjorie?" Everyone laughed, however I was a custom to people laughing or ignoring me.

The first time I ran away from home also involved the church. Phyllis and I attended a Halloween celebration in our church basement, where we ducked for apples in a big grey pail. But since I was little I had to come home early.

Phyllis walked me home, as soon as she left; I went back and peeked in the window where all of the older children were having fun.

I was too little to be out after dark by myself, so I got scared. Walking back home I started crying, I knew I would get a spanking for going back to the church.

It was dark, so I walked on the west side of Albany Avenue near the houses. Finally, I reached Smith Street! It was safer for me to turn here, and then cut across the big lot and take the short cut pass the puddle to Brewster Lane. I would come out near Grandpa's flower garden. If, I went further on Albany Avenue to Brewster Lane, Uncle Hewlett would see me and question me about being out after dark. And I would also have to pass Grandpa's house too.

Finally I got home! I hid in the cab of one of Daddy's dump trucks parked on the lot next to our house and fell a sleep.

My parents said they looked for me for hours! I woke and could hear everyone calling me and got really scared.

When I was found I was thankful. I made like I couldn't talk, but again big tears came down my face. I didn't get a spanking or punished, but I think that it was because my parents were just glad to have found me.

Over the years, I tried to make sense of what the church was teaching me, but I had so many questions. I was always seeking answers! In school I was being taught about how the earth was formed, and in church I was taught how God created the earth. I didn't understand, so Daddy and I had a conversation at the kitchen table one night about God. He explained to me it was not wrong to seek answers and question things. Daddy set the stage for my spiritual seeking!

My other experience with religion was when I attended Bible Class at Mr. and Mrs. Hick's church every Monday after school. This was fun for a few years, because we would color and have parties. Everyone that attended was a relative of mine: Diane Hunter, Christine Hunter, Verna Hicks, and

Janet Gaskins.  Mrs. Hicks also taught piano lessons to some of the children.

Next door was Mrs. Hick's sister-in-law Hilda's red house, and their daughter Verna Hicks was my age.  My only memory of Verna's father Vernon was his making a berry wine from the tree in their front yard.  But the one thing I missed was the baked potato that he cooked in the fireplace outside under the wood and charcoal in his yard for the neighborhood children.

Some of the homes in the community were still using hand-pump for water inside and outside, as well as using the outhouse in their backyard.  Others had converted their hand pump to an electric pump system in their basement.  The pumps would access the underground cool clear streams that ran beneath the surface of North Amityville.

A few outhouses in the neighborhood were Mrs. Hunters, the Devines, Mrs. Clarks, the Broadnicks, and the one at Aunt Graces's house.  All the homes had bathroom, but the children were not allowed to use them. I don't eat rhubarb today, since it always grew near the outhouses.

# Chapter 35

# Mama

Mama was into raising child, and Daddy was into his construction business. And I don't think they had anything else in common, but us kids. My mother didn't understand why my father played golf or working so hard.

As a teenager, Daddy was a caddie at the same Bethpage Public Golf Course, where the U. S. Open is held. From North Amityville, he and other colored teenagers would walk towards Bethpage hoping to be picked up by an early morning golfer. After World War II, Daddy played golf every Sunday, and sometime during the week. He loved the game! He taught Phyllis and me how to hold the golf club, and we would hit balls from our backyard over the path into the woods behind our house.

Mama didn't have many friends or interest of her own. Her children were her life! She never worked until after my parents separated in the late 1960s, and that was just for a few years. She was raised to get married and be a wife, as well as a mother. I guess she was good at it, since four of us got college educations, and my brother is an excellent craftsman.

My mother never talked much about her childhood.  I know she spent part of her life on Sprague Ave with Grandpa Scurlock's sister Aunt Lil, and lived briefly on Great Neck Road with her Grandma and step-grandfather Mr. Miller.

One story Mama told me was that her grandparents had a parrot that would say, "The children did it!"  The children were Junior, Irma, and Wilda.

I never heard my mother talk about spending anytime with her parents.  But in later years, my grandmother and mother were best friends, who saw each other everyday.

Aunt Lil was Mama's favorite aunt and the one that raised her cousin Sonny.  She also babysat for Phyllis and me.  She would tell us stories about growing up in Fayetteville, North Carolina, and give us a tour of the family treasures she kept hidden in her trunk.  I wish I could remember the details of these stories!

During thunder and lightening storms Mama would cover the mirrors with towels, put the silverware away, make sure there was no water around, and we would sit in the living room until the storm was over.  Later I figured it out; Mama must have been in a house that was struck by lightening during her childhood.

I lived 17-years with my mother, but I know very little about her accept that her friends were Benny Henry, Hannah

Hunter Gaskin, the Bryant sisters, and Ismay Bean. However, I know she is a descendant of a long line of strong colored women!

# Chapter 36

# Post World War II

After the War, Bill would give my mother Wilda money each week to run the house. She would get extra money for school clothes, holidays, and just because she asked. And she never had to pay any household bills. My mother always had the family car, and never had to drive Daddy's pickup truck.

First, there was the Nash that got stuck on the railroad tracks, then the big gray Buick with the running boards and armrest that divided the back seat. We would pull the armrest down and sit on it. We got this car in summer of 1950, Hodgie was a baby, and would always be sitting on my lap. The cars back then did not have seat belts!

One afternoon, Daddy was driving us back from Aunt Lil's funeral at Powell's Funeral Home, as he made the turn from Albany Ave. unto Brewster Lane, the right-side back door opened and I fell out holding Hodgie in my arms. We rolled down the hill towards Mrs. Franklin's house and got a little scratched and bruised. I have never forgotten being frightened as we rolled over-and-over.

Our big trip with the new car was to pick Phyllis up from the Girl Scout Camp Eddy on the eastern end of the

Island. The colored Girl Scout Troop had spent a week at the camp, but I was just a Brownie and could not attend.

Mama and Daddy also had friends that we would visit in Dick Hills, and we would ride to Riverhead in our new cars. Daddy would drive us pass the duck farms, which you could smell, as well as the sod and potato fields. There wasn't much else to see, so he would show us the mental hospitals: Northport, Islip and Kings Park. They were the largest buildings on the island.

In later years, I found out that some of these trips were to see Daddy's brother Paul at the Northport Veterans Hospital. Paul like Daddy had enlisted in the service during World War II, but he suffered from being shell-shocked.

I think being shell-shocked was when a soldier, who was stunned by the constant bombing, became distressed and exhausted by the prolonged trauma of the war. But my Grandpa Brewster was a shame and would not sign Paul out of the Veterans hospital, when it became time for him to be released.

A year old two-toned gray Buick without running boards followed around the Christmas of 1952. Our getting the car had something to do with hitting the numbers - the colored peoples' Lotto! Daddy was a friend of the numbers banker, who owned part of the grocery store across from where we caught the school bus at the corner of Smith Street and Albany Avenue.

It was a great Christmas! Hodgie was about three years old and got a set of Lionel Trains, and a Hopalong Cassidy cowboy suit.

The Lionel train set covered the entire floor of our upstairs back bedrooms. It had a cargo station with cows that made sounds, street lights that shown bright, mountains, and bridges. I loved to watch when the train pulled into the station and a train man would push large grey cans marked milk onto a platform.

Daddy, Phyllis and I played for hours with Hodgie's trains; however he never got a chance too. By the time he was old enough the trains were packed away deep in the attic.

After the Buicks came the station wagons, a few Fords and the cars that had to be hot-wired to start.

During this period, I only remember my father being involved in two big family decisions. One was when we got our first black and white television to see Jackie Robinson and the Dodges play. The other was when he built the garage and breezeway onto our house.

The night before he stared construction, Phyllis and I were watching television as Daddy sketched a picture of the breezeway and the garage. The next morning the bricks were delivered to our driveway and the project was started. Daddy organized his office in the breezeway, and repaired his trucks in our large garage.

I always worried that my father did not eat right, I never saw him eat breakfast, but heard that on Sunday, Daddy, Uncle Robert and Uncle Dave would have breakfast at a diner before playing golf at Bethpage on their famous Black course.

Uncle Dave was my father's sister Sarah's first husband. During my early childhood, they lived in the south, but returned after the war to Huntington, and Aunt Sara went to work at Republic Aviation and Uncle Dave at Grumman Aviation.

Daddy left early every morning seven days a week and mama never made his lunch. She would save food on the stove for his dinner. But Mama was tired!

For a very short time Daddy paid Phyllis and me to make his lunch. I would bet anything that he didn't eat the lunches, since most were peanut butter and jelly sandwiches.

Our family always ate supper around 6 o'clock accept on Sunday when we sat down to eat dinner at 3 pm. Phyllis and I would be home from Sunday school, and Daddy home from playing golf. We had chicken or pot roast on Sunday, beans and franks on Wednesday, spaghetti on Thursday and eels, clams, crabs or flounder on Friday. Monday and Tuesday, we had hamburgers, leftovers or meatloaf. Most of our meals came with mash potatoes, string beans, kernel, or cream corn. Our diet was similar to the early Long Island Indians ancestors.

Sometime I would help my mother "pop" string beans for dinner. Grandpa, also the Broadnicks raised string beans, lettuce, tomatoes, eggplant, and corn, so we had a lot of fresh vegetables. On other occasions, I plucked the chickens before Mama fried, boiled or baked them.. Even the chickens from the A & P had to have their small feathers plucked.

Our Sunday dinner treat was corn on the cob, baked potato, or candied yams. We had two exotic meals during my childhood. One was venison (deer) and the other was swab (baby pigeons). Our meals were really predictable growing up.

Once a year, Mama would cook black-eyed peas, collard greens, egg potato salad, and pickled pig feet on New Years Eve. She said, "It was for good luck!" I learned later, that this was a black southern tradition Mama got from the Scurlocks. But we never thought of ourselves as having southern relatives, we were Long Island Indians, or colored people!

# Chapter 37

# Our Dahlia Garden

From age 6 to 10 years old, life was very lonely! Mama didn't have time for me! She was having children every two years until I was ten, and she was always tired. Daddy was an entrepreneur working constantly with his construction business, and getting home late. Phyllis had her own friends and did not have time for her younger sister.

I tried hanging out with our neighbor Janet Gaskins, who was a cousin. Her mother Hannah Hunter Gaskins was the daughter of Ernest and Katherine Hunter. But one day Janet was sent to live with her other Grandmother in Philadelphia, PA.

Grandpa Scurlock was Mama's father; however Daddy's father was just Grandpa. Once Grandpa moved back to North Amityville after the war, he became such an important part of my life.

My friend Grandpa would get up and leave every morning around 5:30 AM because he said, "the early bird gets the worms." Some mornings, I would watch him walk pass our house to the path.

Grandpa was getting bald; he would always say "Grass does not grow on a busy street." Every night I would sit on our fence near the path waiting for him to come home between 6 and 7 o'clock.

Grandpa would walk from the Amityville Railroad Station, up Broadway, and then cut through the woods taking the path near Hunter Court, Devine Place, and the boundary of our backyard. He would always have a piece of candy or gum for me. On special occasions Grandpa brought fresh hand-packed Breyer's vanilla ice cream from Fisher's Ice Cream Parlor in the village. He received a gold watch for 30-years of serve when he retired from driving for the U. S. Trucking Company near the New York City docks.

During the spring and summer, he would pay me for sprinkling limestone and peat moss on his dahlia bulbs, and later to pick the dead flowers. About three weeks after school started, I would begin to help grandpa throw the dead plants into the old fishpond.

"Gal," he said, "these old plants will be fertilizer or mulch for next year." The following year after spreading the limestone, Grandpa and I would spread the new mulch.

The dahlia garden was beautiful! If fact, Grandpa's dahlias were mentioned and pictured in the *American Home Magazine*, and he also won a blue ribbon from the New York Dahlia Society. The ribbon was won for a red and white dahlia named after his second wife called "Gladys."

Daddy said, when he was young, Grandpa would sell flowers at the New York City flower market downtown near the docks. Now, it was a hobby for him.

Every Labor Day weekend, our family would go to the Shinnecock Pow Wow. But the Sunday before we would go to the Pow wow, members of the New York Dahlia Society would come out to North Amityville to visit Grandpa and his dahlia gardens. Phyllis and I would watch the beautiful men and women with their shinny cars visit. They would have sandwiches without the crust, fancy cookies and punch. Grandma Gladys would serve martinis when Grandpa was not looking. They would walk through Grandpa and my garden, as they said, "oh" and "ah" at his flowers.

Aunt Helen, Aunt Eva and Big Helen were all allowed to attend the party. But, my mother, Bill, Phyllis, the babies and me would watch from the end of Brewster Lane.

When the last car pulled out of Grandpa's yard, Phyllis and I would be allowed to join him and hear all about the party. Grandma Gladys would give us sandwiches without crust, fancy cookies and punch on the porch, and we would be told how beautiful Aunt Helen and Aunt Eva looked.

Sometime, Big Helen, Grandma Gladys' sister would be painting with oil on the front lawn. Upon arrival she would always have her easel and oil paints with her. She painted a picture of grandpa's house, the big tree in the front yard, and another of the dahlias named Gladys. I loved to watch her paint, so she would take the time to explain the process.

Sometime our private party would include Aunt Helen playing jacks with us. Aunt Eva was a college student in Oklahoma City, and playing jacks was beneath her. Later, she taught French in college, and traveled to Africa, where she contacted a rare bone disease that caused her early death.

Phyllis, Cousin Margie, Aunt Helen and Aunt Eva set examples of what women could accomplish, and were my early mentors.

# Chapter 38

## Mama's Best Friend

After World War II, all the colored families still had beautiful flower and healthy vegetable gardens in the summer. Our relatives and friends brought us fresh vegetables, as well as Phyllis and I grew radishes, onions, cucumbers, and carrots in a small garden and baked dirt mud cookies in the sun. And it was during the summer my mother taught me that friendship was important.

Every year Benny Nelson Henry, who had stood up for my parents when they got married would visit for at least two weeks.

Daddy would drive to the Bronx and pick Benny, her husband Gene and daughter Barbara up from 218th Street and White Plains Road. Later, their dog and new baby Elaine would also come to North Amityville.

If, Daddy was unable to pick Benny's family up, they would travel from New York City by the Long Island Railroad, and we would meet them at the Amityville train station. But Mama would not miss a summer without her best friend!

After Benny's parents died in Charleston, South Carolina, she moved to Amityville with her uncle Rev. James

Henry Thomas and his wife Sara (Sadie), her mother's sister. And Mama and Benny became teenage friends.

In the Bronx, the Henrys lived in a small three room apartment in walking distance to the elevated subway. They were city people!

For two weeks, Barbara and I would get to play together, while the adults ordered Chinese food (Egg Foo Yung, and Pepper Steak). But the children would just get Chicken Chow Mein. This made me think that Egg Foo Yung and Pepper Steak were uniquely cooked for adults.

They also cook barbeque, or the clams, crabs, and flounder that the men brought back on one of their many fishing trips. In the evening, the adults would play cards!

Each summer was great, since Mama was so happy to have Benny visit, and Daddy loved to fish with Gene.

Benny and my mother would remain friends for over 70-years.

# Chapter 39

# Amityville Public School System

The kindergarten room was in the lower level of the Park Central School in the Village of Amityville. In the middle of the room was a raised pond with gold fish. In kindergarten, we spend a lot of time on lines to go to the water fountain, bathroom, or outdoors. I don't remember much about going to Kindergarten except that Christine and Diane Hunter, and I were in the same class. I was also too young to go to first grade, so I had to spend another semester in Kindergarten.

Rena Smith, daughter of Fred Smith, who had the taxi business drove the cab that took Christine and me to school each day.

When we finally got to 1st grade, it was being held in an Annex Building. The building was a long white washed building with a large playground built on cement. The entire building had a chain link fence around it. I think the building had something to do with World War II.

The school year was split into A and B sessions, and you would graduate from one to the other. I remember the monkey bars, seesaw, and swings. I was not very athletic and hated to participate on the equipment. One day when

Christine, Diane and I were using the seesaw, Diane jumped off and caused me to come down hard on the cement. I never wanted to ride the seesaw again.

Phyllis and I did not take our lunch, because Mama was having babies and did not have time to fix it. I would buy the hot lunch for $0.25. The lunch would include milk, which I never drank, a hot plate of unidentifiable meat, surplus can vegetables left over from World War II, and a piece of sheet cake or fruit for dessert.

The schools did not offer breakfast, but in the morning we got a cup of orange juice, and in the afternoon cookies and milk. I loved volunteering to pass out the cookies and milk.

I think my first grade teacher's name was Mrs Hayes. She might have been Phyllis' 1$^{st}$ grade teacher too.

During the three years spent at the Annex, I learned to write my name, add, and subtract. We read *Jim and Judy* over and over again. And the teachers used flash cards to teach us multiplication and division.

At the end of the day, we would leave the fenced area and line up for the school buses to go home.

During these years, I had a white school friend, who lived on the Broadway end of Smith Street. I think my mother had gone to school with her parents.

By the fourth grade, we moved to the Park North Building. And she moved to the Village of Amityville and her white friends.

Park North was a building that was built in the late 1890s and was the first building to house integrated classes. My Grandpa Job, my father, mother, and Phyllis had all attended school here. In fact, Charles Devine Brewster lead the integration of the Amityville Public School System the year the building was built, and the colored Huntington School # 6 was closed for good!

My 4$^{th}$ grade teacher was Miss Sanford, and she remains my favorite teacher. And my violin teacher Mrs. Lush had attended school with my mother. I loved the way the violin sounded, but could not master playing it.

My report cards all said, "Nice girl, I wish there were more like her". This was my favorite year in school. I was quite, and sort of smart, but could not see the black or green boards well. Letters and words were always fuzzy. My report cards said, I was such a well-mannered and sweet child, I got by without seeing the blackboard and having glasses. I had also learned how to be invisible to the teachers!

The next year, we were back in the Park Central School, where I had started kindergarten on the lower level. Our classroom was the old junior high science room of Mr. Hicks.

My fifth grade teacher was Ms Bergman, a first-year teacher with something to prove. Towards the end of the year, she asked me to give an oral report, but when I did not speak loud she slapped me in the face. I can still hear her yelling at me, "talk loud enough, so Jimmy Goodman can hear you in the back of the room." When I didn't she told me, "to shout, so Mr. Dayton could hear me in his office." I started crying; when she slapped me I knocked her books off her desk. She grabbed me and locked me in the coat closet, and took the class out to the play ground. I stayed in the dark closet until another teacher heard me crying and found me.

Ms Bergman did not teach long in the Amityville School System   For the rest of my public school education, I never had to stand in front of the classroom again.

Phyllis was in junior high school and it had been moved to the old high school building Park South, and the high school moved to Merrick Road. The high school was now the Amityville Memorial High School, a new building built in the early 1950s. My cousins Margie and Donald were both in school there.

When school got out the buses would line up near the Park South building. First, the Park Central students, and then the Park South students would get on the buses. As a 5<sup>th</sup> grade student I took the early buses and Phyllis' bus followed.

This was the year that the bus driver tried to molest me on the bus. He tried to kiss me as I was getting off the bus, and I started crying. Some of the children on the bus ran to Phyllis' bus that followed and got her. My big sister jumped on the bus, kicking and spitting at the driver, who never bothered me again. I also think my father had a "come home to Jesus" conversation with the driver that evening.

Air raid drills were part of everyday life for schoolchildren in the late 1940s and
early '50s. Children were taught to "duck and cover"
under their desks and were herded
into school basements for periodic air raid drills.

Source: wais.stanford.edu

# Chapter 40

# Duck and Cover

My brother Hodgie was born just after Jackie Robinson, and the Dodge were in the play-offs, and Daddy brought our first television. And at Republic Aviation, the jet planes were breaking the sound barrior over our house.

When Mama went to Brunswick Hospital to have Hodgie, Phyllis and I were left at Aunt Lil's house on the corner of Sprague Avenue and Albany Avenue. She had a one bedroom second floor apartment. We had also been left at Aunt Lil's, when Daddy riding a motorcycle hit a brick wall and broke his jaw.

The doctors wired Daddy's jaw together and he was only allowed to eat baby food. But after a week, he organized Phyllis and I to sneak him solid food. Mama caught the three of us!

The new baby Hodgie replaced my dolls! I pushed his carriage and carried him everywhere.

My next sister was born just before America went to war again. She was one of the prettiest babies I had seen. She was so quite! It was like she was not there.

Soon after she was born America entered another the *forgotten* Korean War, which was fought between June 25,

1950 with a cease-fire on July 27, 1953. It was a war fought between North Korea and South Korea, the partitioned states of Korea  or the Soviet and the United States occupation zones after World War II. And the young colored men of North Amityville went overseas again!

At the end of World War II, the United States had detonated the Atomic Bomb on Hiroshima August 6 and Nagasaki on August 9, 1945, and anything flammable burned for 3-miles. The fallout was radioactive particles felling on the area when it rained. This caused the U. S. to fear that during the Korean War an Atomic Bomb would be used on our country.

I remember our school received a comic books featuring a cartoon turtle called *Bert* that urged them to "*duck and cover*" in the event of an atomic strike. So with the help of *Bert*, I duck and covered through elementary school and the Korean War.

Every week or a couple of times a month, we ducked and covered at our desk or in the halls of Amityville Public Schools.

The air raid signal at the fire houses would blast in Amityville, and everyone had to leave the streets. They ducked and covered at home and at work.

Daddy built a few bomb shelters for white families, and everyone stock piled can goods.

We ducked and covered, when my brother Hodgie and sister fought off measles and the chicken pox at the same time. She was so small and young that Dr. Paddock tied small socks on her hands, so she would not scratch the scabs.

Dr. Paddock was our school doctor, as well as our family doctor. He would visit our home and charge Mama just $5.00. He would give us pills in little white boxes. Mama said he had inherited the pills from his uncle. When the air raid signal sounded Dr. Paddock ducked and covered.

We ducked and covered, when my youngest sister was born. Now, there were three babies in our household, and America was being warned of the "industrial military complex."

# Chapter 41

## I became a Negro

By the time I entered Junior High School in the Park South building, I was no longer an Indian or Colored girl, I had become a Negro. I don't know when it happened, but the white children that had taken the school bus with us no longer did.

I still sat in the front of the bus, now the New York City colored veterans children gathered in the back. The older teachers that taught my parents still referred to me as colored or Indian, but the new teachers called us "Negro."

On May 17, 1954, the Supreme Court ruled on the landmark case Browns vs. Board of Education of Topeka, Kansas, unanimously agreeing that segregation in public schools is unconstitutional. But I didn't think our school was segregated. I learned later that I was wrong!

The following year, Dec. 1, 1955, in Montgomery, Alabama, Rosa Parks refuses to give up her seat at the front of the "colored section" of a bus to a white passenger. In response to her arrest the Montgomery black community launched a bus boycott, which lasted for more than a year, until the buses were desegregated Dec. 21, 1956. The Civil Rights Movement had begun, right after I began high school.

I made a career choice when I entered high school in 1956, and had decided to become an architect, since I loved reading my father's blueprints. By the end of my first year, I wanted to take drafting, but found out that girls were not allowed in the class. After a discussion with my father, the guidance counselor let me signup for the drafting class for my sophomore year.

The class started and I was placed in the front of the room at a drafting desk. The male students did not talk to me. This was the first time I can remember feeling different, because of my race and my sex.

I went through my high school years as a Negro, but my family remained colored and Indian, and would attend the Shinnecock Indian Pow Wow each Labor Day weekend. And Chief Thunderbird still visited my grandfather at 63 Brewster Lane. And Grandpa still told us stories about our Indian heritage and Yamaqua!

I was born a Long Island Indian with strong roots to the area; who later found out I was Colored, Negro, Black, African American, and finally Native American in a town that defined my life.

I was born to a family with a rich heritage. In a world I have never understood, but find I am doomed to live out my life as God planned.